Strategies to Integrate the Arts in Science

Authors

Vivian Poey, M.F.A.
Nicole Weber, Ph.D.
Gene Diaz, Ph.D.
Sam Smiley, M.F.A.

LESLEY UNIVERSITY

SHELL EDUCATION

Publishing Credits

Dona Herweck Rice, *Editor-in-Chief*; Robin Erickson, *Production Director*;
Lee Aucoin, *Creative Director*; Timothy J. Bradley, *Illustration Manager*;
Sara Johnson, M.S.Ed., *Editorial Director*; Tracy Edmunds, *Editor*;
Leah Quillian, *Assistant Editor*; Grace Alba, *Designer*;
Corinne Burton, M.A.Ed., *Publisher*

Series Editors

Linda Dacey, Ed.D. Professor of Education and Mathematics, Lesley University
Lisa Donovan, Ph.D., Associate Professor, Massachusetts College of Liberal Arts, Fine and Performing Arts

Contributing Authors

David Williams, M.Ed., Grade 4 Teacher, Newbury Elementary School, MA
Alyson Marcel, Graduate Student, Masters in Art Therapy at Lesley University

Consultants

William Barowy, Ph.D., Associate Professor of Science and Technology in Education Programs, Lesley
    University
Louise Pascale, Ph.D. Associate Professor, Creative Arts in Learning, Lesley University
Meg Lippert, Director of Storytelling, Homer learning website and Adjunct Faculty, Creative Arts in
    Learning, Lesley University
Celeste Miller, Adjunct Faculty, Lesley University Creative Arts in Learning Division

Image Credits
All images Shutterstock

Standards
© 2004 Mid-continent Research for Education and Learning (McREL)
© 2007 Teachers of English to Speakers of Other Languages, Inc. (TESOL)
© 2007 Board of Regents of the University of Wisconsin System. World-Class Instructional Design and Assessment
    (WIDA). For more information on using the WIDA ELP Standards, please visit the WIDA website at www.wida.us.
© 2010 National Governors Association Center for Best Practices and Council of Chief State School Officers (CCSS)

Shell Education
5301 Oceanus Drive
Huntington Beach, CA 92649-1030
http://www.shelleducation.com
ISBN 978-1-4258-1086-3
© 2013 Shell Educational Publishing, Inc.

Table of Contents

The Importance of Arts Integration

Teachers have an important and challenging job, and it seems that they are asked to do more with each passing year. Lesley University professors in the Creative Arts Division hear from teachers regularly that integrating the arts would be a great thing to do if they just had time and support. Yet research shows that integration of the arts is an efficient and effective strategy for addressing some of the greatest challenges in today's educational landscape as the arts deepen learning in ways that engage all learners of all abilities and needs (President's Committee on the Arts and the Humanities 2011; Burnaford 2007). Study after study points to compelling evidence of the significant outcomes that are linked to arts integration.

According to the President's Committee on the Arts and the Humanities, "studies have now documented significant links between arts integration models and academic and social outcomes for students, efficacy for teachers, and school-wide improvements in culture and climate. Arts integration is efficient, addressing a number of outcomes at the same time. Most important, the greatest gains in schools with arts integration are often seen school-wide and also with the most hard-to-reach and economically disadvantaged students" (2011).

A recent study funded by the Ford Foundation and led by researchers from Lesley University's Creative Arts in Learning Division and an external advisory team conducted research with over 200 Lesley alumni teaching across the country who had been trained in arts-integration strategies. The findings suggest that arts-integrated teaching provides a variety of strategies for accessing content and expressing understanding of learning that is culturally responsive and relevant in students' lives. This leads to deep learning, increased student ownership, and engagement with academic content. Not only does arts integration engage students in creativity, innovation, and imagination, it renews teachers' commitment to teaching (Bellisario and Donovan with Prendergast 2012).

Really, then, the question becomes this: *How can we afford to not provide students with access to the arts as an engaging way to learn and to express ideas across the curriculum?*

Arts integration is the investigation of curricular content through artistic explorations where the arts provide an avenue for rigorous investigation, representation, expression, and reflection of both curricular content and the art form itself (Diaz, Donovan, and Pascale 2006). This book provides teachers with concrete strategies to integrate the arts across the curriculum. Arts-integration strategies are introduced with contextual information about the art form (creative movement, drama, music, poetry, storytelling, and visual arts).

The Importance of Arts Integration *(cont.)*

Each art form provides you with new ways to help students fully engage with content and participation in memorable learning experiences. Creative movement allows students to embody ideas and work conceptually. Drama challenges students to explore multiple perspectives of characters, historical figures, and scientists. Music develops students' ability to listen, to generate a sense of community, and to communicate and connect aurally. Poetry invites students to build a more playful, fresh relationship to written and spoken language. Storytelling connects students with roots in the oral tradition and heightens their awareness of the role stories play in their lives. Visual art taps into students' ability to observe critically, to envision, to think through metaphor, and to build visual literacy in a world where images are pervasive.

Providing learners with the opportunity to investigate concepts and to express their understanding with the powerful languages of the arts will deepen students' understanding, heighten their curiosity, and bring forward their voices as they interact more fully with content and translate their ideas into new forms. This book is a beginning, a "way in."

We invite you to see for yourself by bringing the strategies shared in this book to your classroom and seeing what happens. We hope this resource leaves you looking for deeper experiences with the arts both for you and for your students.

What Does It Mean to Integrate the Arts?

We believe that a vital element necessary in establishing a learning environment that fosters artistic creativity and evokes scientific curiosity and exploration can be found in the integration of the arts and science. Active involvement in the arts can help learners in science and other fields explore different perspectives and internalize new ideas and ways of thinking.

The beauty of the world that we know through the study of science is often missing in our lessons as we share information and require students to engage in the scientific method as a mandate. When we integrate science with the arts in our teaching, learning becomes multisensory, gains relevance, and we add joy to the experience. Students build on their own curiosity. The arts provide a vivid and dynamic context in which learners can wrestle with scientific ideas, scientific methods, and scientific reasoning.

You might think that engagement with the arts and the sciences is reserved for the few who have been given special gifts, those who have rare expertise. But this is not the case—you do not need to be an artist or a scientist to add this teaching approach to your repertoire. While we encourage collaboration with arts specialists across disciplines and grade levels, we also want to emphasize this point. No special abilities or talents are needed except for the willingness to begin!

The Importance of Arts Integration *(cont.)*

There are many connections between the arts and the sciences. For example, architects, sculptors, and musicians must rely on scientific knowledge every day in physics, chemistry, biology, and earth sciences. There are times in the science classroom when the arts are used to introduce or culminate the study of a specific topic. Some teachers may already have favorite lessons in which mobile sculptures become solar systems or lessons in which children learn to dance the growth of a tree. What we are aiming for here, though, is a seamless blending of the two areas in a sustained manner. We will guide you in the use of the arts and provide a context in which scientific concepts take shape and deepen while the arts inform and enrich the lives of your students. This is not just for enrichment but also for a change in practice that allows you to create your own path into arts integration. We want you to use arts integration as an approach to teaching the most prevalent standards in your science curriculum and to do so frequently. When scientific ideas are taught through artistic explorations, students develop skills and knowledge in both disciplines. We will share strategies with you that are flexible enough to be used across content strands and grade levels.

With our current curricula dominated by reading and mathematics, little room is left for the arts and sciences. Yet as educators, we want to teach the whole child. Students need both the arts and academic disciplines. Research suggests that academic achievement may be linked to the arts (Kennedy 2006). As noted by Douglas Reeves (2007), "the challenge for school leaders is to offer every student a rich experience with the arts without sacrificing the academic opportunities students need" (80). By integrating the arts with the sciences, we are able to place scientific ideas within rich settings *and* provide our students with access to the arts. In fact, the arts can lead to "deep learning" (Bellisario and Donovan with Prendergast 2012) where students are more genuinely engaged with academic content, spend more time on task, and take ownership of their learning while deepening their imaginative and creative skills.

Why Should I Integrate the Arts?

Mathematics and science are frequently linked together in schools, with STEM (Science, Technology, Engineering, and Mathematics) initiatives formalizing this association. While we applaud STEM efforts, we seek to expand the potential for other interdisciplinary connections. The arts also offer particular advantages for learning that should not be ignored. In a briefing on changing STEM to STEAM with the inclusion of the arts, John Maeda, president of the Rhode Island School of Design, noted that STEM would benefit by adding the arts and design to trigger more innovation (Rhode Island School of Design 2011). Beth Baker (2012) states that "innovation happens through science, technology, engineering, and mathematics. Could it be missing something that is actually quite important? It's missing the arts—the right-brain innovation that has propelled our country, made us competitive" (253).

The Importance of Arts Integration (cont.)

Rinne et al. (2011) identify several ways in which arts integration improves long-term retention through elaboration, enactment, and rehearsal. Specifically, when learners create and add details to their own visual models, dramatize a concept or skill, sing a song repeatedly, or rehearse for a performance, they are increasing the likelihood that they will remember what they have learned. This retention lasts not just for the next chapter test but over significant periods of time. Through repetition that doesn't feel like "drill and kill," this information is retained for life because students become deeply engaged when working in arts integration. They eagerly revisit, review, rehearse, edit, and work through ideas repeatedly and in authentic ways as they translate ideas into new forms.

As brain research deepens our understanding of how learning takes place, educators have come to better appreciate the importance of the arts. The arts support communication, emotional connections, community, and higher-order thinking. They are also linked to increased academic achievement, especially among at-risk students. Eric Jensen (2001) argues that the "arts enhance the process of learning. The systems they nourish, which include our integrated sensory, attentional, cognitive, emotional, and motor capabilities, are, in fact, the driving forces behind all other learning" (2). Lessons and activities that integrate science and the arts provide a rich environment for the exploration of scientific ideas for all students and particularly for those students who need new ways to access curriculum and to express understanding as well as providing another source of motivation.

Teaching through the arts provides authentic differentiated learning for every student in the classroom. As neurologist Todd Rose notes (2012), all learners learn in variable ways. The Center for Applied Special Technology (2012) suggests that in meeting the needs of variable learners, educators should expand their teaching to provide universal design. That is, that teachers include strategies that "are flexible and responsive to the needs of all learners" by providing "multiple means of engagement, methods of presentation of content, and multiple avenues for expression of understanding." The integration of the arts provides opportunities to address universal design principles. Arts integration not only benefits students by deepening their connection to content and fostering interdisciplinary learning in the arts and science but also promotes what the Partnership for 21st Century Skills (2011) researchers note as the 4Cs: creativity, critical thinking, communication, and collaboration. Arts integration brings these significant benefits to learning and also engages teachers and students in curiosity, imagination, and passion for learning.

Arts and the Standards

Essential Qualities in a Science Program

The National Research Council of the National Academies (National Research Council 2012) states that science teaching and learning are powerful when built around three major dimensions that include:

1. Scientific and engineering practices

2. Crosscutting concepts

3. Core ideas within four disciplinary areas (physical science; life science; earth and space science; and engineering, technology, and application of science)

The science and engineering practices reflect how professionals work in the field and directly relate to artistic processes. The crosscutting concepts further aid in providing an organizational framework that helps students connect interdisciplinary knowledge in a meaningful way to understand the world from a scientific point of view. These concepts include patterns; cause and effect; scale, proportion, and quantity; systems and system models; energy and matter; structure and function; and stability and change. We believe that integration with the arts supports a deeper understanding of the general science practices, crosscutting concepts, and content knowledge within the local environmental context where possible. The model lessons in this book were developed with these goals in mind.

Artistic Habits of Mind

As well as essential qualities of science programs, students will also be developing these artistic habits of mind (Hetland et al. 2007). With these habits of mind, students are able to:

1. Develop craft	5. Observe
2. Engage and persist	6. Reflect
3. Envision	7. Stretch and explore
4. Express	8. Understand the art world

Though these habits were identified in an investigation of visual art practices, they are relevant for the practice of all of the arts. As students engage in science through these lenses, their understanding will deepen. They will become active participants in making meaning, discussing ideas, and reflecting on their learning.

It is important to note that the skills the arts help develop are valued in every field. The arts develop these skills naturally as students explore and translate ideas into artistic form. Researcher Lois Hetland notes that "it is these qualities—intrinsic to the arts— that are valued in every domain but not necessarily taught in those subjects in school. That's what makes the arts such potent resources for teaching valued dispositions— what the arts teach well is not used uniquely in the arts but is valuable across a wide spectrum of contexts" (2009, 37).

Arts and the Standards *(cont.)*

Classroom Environment

A safe classroom environment is needed for scientific ideas and artistic expressions to flourish. Learners must feel comfortable to make mistakes, to critique the work of others, and to celebrate success. Think back to groups to which you have presented new ideas or creative works. How did you feel as you waited for their reactions? What was it about their behavior that made you feel more or less comfortable? What was it about your thinking that made you feel more or less safe? Such reflections will lead you to ways you can talk about these ideas with your students. As teachers, we must be role models for our students as we model our willingness to take risks and engage in new ways of learning. You will find that the arts by their nature invite risk taking, experimentation, and self-discipline as well as encourage the development of a supportive learning community.

Developing a learning community in which learners support and respect one another takes time, but there are things that you can do to help support its development:

- **Establish clear expectations for respect**. Respect is nonnegotiable. As students engage in creative explorations, it is crucial that they honor one another's ideas, invite all voices to the table, and discuss the work in ways that value each contribution. Self-discipline and appreciation for fellow students' creative work is often a beneficial outcome of arts integration (Bellisario and Donovan with Prendergast 2012). Take time for students to brainstorm ways in which they can show one another respect and what they can do when they feel that they have not been respected. Work with students to create guidelines for supporting the creative ideas of others and agree to uphold them as a group.

- **Explore several ice breakers** during the first weeks of school that allow students to get to know one another informally and begin to discover interests they have in common. As students learn more about one another, they develop a sense of themselves as individuals as well as a classroom unit and are more apt to want to support one another. Using fun, dynamic warm-ups not only helps students get their brains working but also builds a sense of community and support for risk taking.

- **Tell your students about ways in which you are engaged in learning new ideas**. Talk about your realizations and challenges along the way and demonstrate your own willingness to take risks and persevere.

Arts and the Standards (*cont.*)

- **Find ways to support the idea that we can all act, draw, sing, rhyme, and so forth**. Avoid saying negative things about your own arts or science skill levels, and emphasize your continuous growth.

- **Learn to ask open-ended questions rather than give answers**. By asking a question such as "What does this symbol represent to you?," students are able to refocus or clarify their own thinking.

- **Avoid judgments**. Students who are trying to earn your praise for their artistic products will not take the risks necessary for creative work. Encourage students to reflect on their own goals and whether they think they have met them.

- **Emphasize process over product**. Enormous learning and discovery takes place during the creative process. This is as significant as the final product that is produced and in some cases even more so.

How This Book Is Organized

Strategies

The strategies and model lessons in this book are organized within six art modalities:

- creative movement

- drama

- music

- poetry

- storytelling

- visual arts

Within each modality, five strategies are presented that integrate that art form with the teaching of the sciences. The strategies are not intended as an exhaustive list but rather as exemplary ways to integrate the arts into the sciences.

Though we have provided a model lesson for each strategy, these strategies are flexible and can be used in a variety of ways across a variety of content areas. These models will allow you to try out the ideas with your students and to envision many other ways to adapt these strategies for use in your teaching. For example, in the drama strategy of teacher-in-role, we emphasized design engineering of transportation, but you may prefer to integrate it with other areas of science or STEM, such as cell biology (where the teacher takes on the role of a cell biologist) or geology. Also note that strategies can be implemented across the art forms. For example, the strategy of juxtaposition could be associated with any of the arts as we can juxtapose movements, characters, sounds, words, perspectives, or materials. Furthermore, as you become more familiar and comfortable with the strategies, you may combine a variety of them across the art modalities within one lesson. For example, you might have students begin with creative movement to explore organic materials, then dramatize experts in the field finding examples of organic materials and listing the terms and characteristics they associate with those materials, and finally, use those words as "found words" to write a poem. The goal is to make the choices that best fit you and your students.

How This Book Is Organized *(cont.)*

Organization of the Lessons

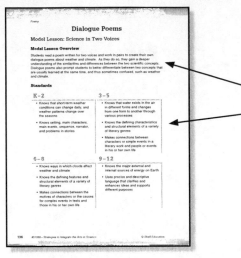

Each model lesson begins with an **overview**, followed by the list of **standards** addressed. Note that the standards involve equal rigor for both science and the arts.

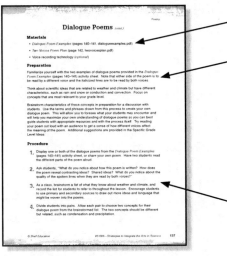

A list of **materials** you will need is provided.

A **preparation** section follows in which ways you can better ensure a successful learning investigation have been identified. Ideas may relate to grouping students, using props to engage learners, or practicing readings with dramatic flair.

The **procedure** section provides step-by-step directions on how to implement the model lesson.

Each model lesson includes **questions** that you can ask as students work. The questions serve to highlight students' scientific reasoning, stimulate their artistic thinking, or debrief their experience.

How This Book Is Organized *(cont.)*

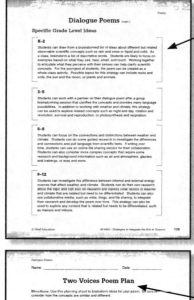

Specific grade level ideas follow with suggestions on how to better meet the needs of students within the K–2, 3–5, 6–8, and 9–12 grade levels. They may also suggest other ways to explore or extend the ideas in the model lesson at these levels. Read all of the sections, as an idea written for a different grade span may suggest something you want to do with your students.

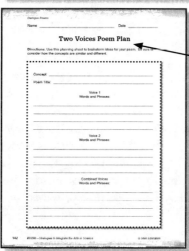

At least one **reproducible** is provided for each model lesson. Often in the form of graphic organizers, the reproducibles are designed to help students brainstorm ideas, organize and record their thinking, or reflect on their learning. Reproducibles are available on the Digital Resource CD in PDF form and oftentimes as Word documents to allow for customization of content and text for students of diverse abilities and needs.

How This Book Is Organized (*cont.*)

How to Use the Lessons

These strategies can be used to teach science in any K–12 classroom with any science curriculum. A strategy lesson can be implemented as a way to deepen or expand the exploration of a topic, or if you have the flexibility, expanded to several days or a week. You may choose to use the strategy lesson within your science lesson, in combination with time assigned to the arts, or when considering storytelling or poetry, perhaps in conjunction with other content areas.

You may wish to focus on one art form at a time in order to become familiar with using that art modality to teach knowledge and skills in science as well as the art form being employed. Or you may want to look through the content index and explore models that relate to what you are teaching now or are about to teach. Over time, you will become familiar with the strategies and find that you choose to integrate them on a regular basis. If integrating arts and science is new to you, consider working with another teacher to explore the ideas together. Collaborate with teachers of art, dance, drama, or music in your school system to draw from their expertise in deepening the artistic work.

Assessment

Data-driven decision making, documentation of learning, and meeting benchmarks are all phrases referring to assessment practices that are embedded in our schools. Assessment has become a time-consuming activity for all involved in education and yet the time and effort spent does not always yield what is needed to improve learning. As you think about how to assess lessons and activities that integrate science and the arts, it is important to stop and consider how to best use assessment to increase learning for your students. It is most likely that in addressing that goal, you will also be documenting learning in ways that can be shared with students, parents, administrators, and other interested stakeholders.

We encourage you to focus on formative assessment, that is, assessment that is incorporated throughout the process of learning. This assessment will inform your instructional decisions during the process of teaching. The purpose of this assessment is to provide feedback for learners and teachers along the way in addition to learning at the end. As such, we are most interested in the data collected during the learning process as well as after it is completed. The goals are to make the learning process visible, to determine the depth of understanding, and to note the process the students undergo as they translate their scientific knowledge into an art form or explore scientific ideas through the arts.

How This Book Is Organized (*cont.*)

There are a variety of tools you can use to gather data to support your instructional decision making:

- **Ask questions to draw out, clarify, and probe students' thinking.** The questions in each strategy section will provide you with ideas on which you can elaborate. Use questioning to make on-the-spot adjustments to your plans as well as to identify learning moments as they are unfolding. This can be as simple as posing a new question or as complex as bringing a few students together for a mini-lesson.

- **Walk around with a clipboard or notebook** so that you can easily capture students' comments and questions as well as your own observations. Too often we think we will remember students' words only to find ourselves unable to reproduce them at a later time. These annotations will allow you to note patterns within a student's remarks or among students' comments. They can suggest misconceptions that provide you with an entry to the next days' work through a comment such as, "Yesterday I noticed that your monologues suggested motivations for your historical figures in science that were different than the texts have shared. Let's talk about how this might be possible based on the sources we have and what you have learned about how history is written." A suggested template is provided in Appendix B (page 251) and available on the Digital Resource CD (notetaking.pdf). Make several copies and attach them to a clipboard.

- **Use the graphic organizers in the model lessons** as support for the creative process. Using these forms, have students brainstorm ideas for their artistic process and their science connections. These organizers provide a snapshot of students' thinking at a point in the creative process.

- **Use a camera to document student learning.** Each of the strategies leads to a creative product but not necessarily one that provides a tangible artifact or one that fits on a standard size piece of paper. Use a digital camera to take numerous pictures that can capture, for example, a piece of visual art at various stages of development or the gestures actors and storytellers use in their dramatic presentations. Similarly, use video to capture planning sessions, group discussions, and final presentations. As well as documenting learning, collecting such evidence helps students reflect back on their learning. Consider developing a learning portfolio for your students that they can review and add to over time.

How This Book Is Organized (cont.)

- Recognize that although each strategy leads to a final creative product, it, too, can be used to inform future instruction. **Comparisons can be made across products to note student growth.**

- **Make students integral parts of the assessment process.** Provide them with opportunities to reflect on their work. For quick, formative reflections, ask students to respond simply. For example, ask them to "move in an unusual way to show a Southern direction." Have students reflect in more complex ways as well. For example, have students choose artifacts to include in their portfolio and explain the reasons for their choices. Have students reflect on their work as a class. For example, ask, "How well did we build on one another's ideas today? How well did we support one another's creative thinking?" Encourage discussion of artistic work to not only draw out what students have learned in their own creative process but also how and what they learn from the work of their peers. In this way, students teach and learn from one another.

- **Design rubrics that help you organize your assessment data.** A well-crafted rubric can help you gather data more quickly as well as increase the likelihood that you are being equitable in your evaluation of assessment data. Select criteria to assess learning in science as well as in the art form because arts integration supports equal rigor both in content and in the arts.

To give you an example of how you could use these strategies in the classroom, consider the collaborative storytelling strategy. In an architecture studio at the Children's Studio School in Washington, DC, students ranging in age from 4 to 6 years old investigated water. They looked at water from various perspectives, including where it comes from, how it gets to us, what it is used for, and how the water cycle works. In Vivian Poey's visual art studio, students investigated the systems at work in getting us what we need. Students immediately brought up water, which had been a big part of their previous learning. As a way of assessing what students already understood about water, the teacher invited students to develop a collaborative story that applied their knowledge in a fantastic fictional account based on what would happen if the Earth's water disappeared.

As students sat in a circle, the teacher provided the beginning of the story: "Once there was an enormous bird flying in outer space. His nose was dry, and his throat was dry. He was so frustrated that he came to the Earth's atmosphere and breathed up all the clouds. Every time the sun evaporated more water, the bird would inhale it again, trying to wet his nose. So the water did not come down." The teacher then invited students to continue that thread to develop the story. One student began, "Down on Earth, there was a boy who had wings. His name was Fred. His arms were inside the wings. He was wearing wingmitts, like mittens but he had wings. But it was not cold, he was just wearing them because he likes to." The story continued to unfold as each individual student added a line:

How This Book Is Organized (cont.)

"Fred was flying and his nose was dry and his throat was dry."

"It was in the sky in the daytime."

"He keeps sniffing and sniffing because no rain is coming."

"His feathers fell because the rain didn't come down."

"The plants died."

"He ate nothing."

"He was going to die."

"He was looking poorer and poorer and poorer, and soon he had no food."

"He realizes that all the plants and the leaves on the tree are gone. And then he goes back and he knows where this is all coming from and he worries it will go on forever."

"Fred took a feather from the bird, and he tickled his nose and the bird sneezed all the water out."

"The water went down the drain."

"The plants growed and growed and growed until they were tall as trees."

"The bird sneezed more water out."

"And the grass growed."

"And Fred's nose got wetter and his throat got clearer and clearer and clearer."

"He flew up in the sky."

"And he ate the grass."

"And he flew up all the way to the clouds."

How This Book Is Organized (cont.)

"And there was never anyone thirsty again."

"And the bird left and went with his family to celebrate because he found home. There is a waterfall and it also rains a lot because it is always spring."

"The end of our book."

In this story, students independently created a main character and took the story to the moment of crisis and through to resolution. The story reflects not only what the students know about water (plants need it to grow and therefore humans need it to drink and also to eat) but also what they know about the structure of stories. In this case, the collaborative storytelling strategy was used as a quick pre-assessment before entering a conversation about systems. It established a good starting point for the conversation and the work to come. Students could then move from the fictional and fantastic to a factual investigation about the complex systems at work. In this case, the questions to ask and investigate can come directly from the story: Why did the plants die? Why do we need plants? How do plants get their water? How do we get our water? Where does our water come from?

As there are many aspects of this task to capture, a rubric can be quite helpful. A suggested rubric is provided in Appendix B (page 252) and on the Digital Resource CD (assessmentrubric.pdf). Observation protocols help teachers document evidence of student learning, something all teachers must do. A variety of forms can be used, and it is not possible to include all areas that you might attend to in an interdisciplinary lesson. Two suggested forms are included in Appendix B, built on the work of Collins (2012a, 2012b) and Dacey (2012a, 2012b, 2012c, 2012d). One form is for use with individual students (page 253, individualform.pdf) and one is for use with groups (page 254, groupform.pdf).

Correlation to the Standards

Shell Education is committed to producing educational materials that are research and standards based. In this effort, we have correlated all of our products to the academic standards of all 50 United States, the District of Columbia, the Department of Defense Dependent Schools, and all Canadian provinces.

How to Find Standards Correlations

To print a customized correlation report of this product for your state, visit our website at http://www.shelleducation.com and follow the on-screen directions. If you require assistance in printing correlation reports, please contact Customer Service at 1-877-777-3450.

Purpose and Intent of Standards

Legislation mandates that all states adopt academic standards that identify the skills students will learn in kindergarten through grade twelve. Many states also have standards for Pre–K. This same legislation sets requirements to ensure the standards are detailed and comprehensive.

Standards are designed to focus instruction and guide adoption of curricula. Standards are statements that describe the criteria necessary for students to meet specific academic goals. They define the knowledge, skills, and content students should acquire at each level. Standards are also used to develop standardized tests to evaluate students' academic progress. Teachers are required to demonstrate how their lessons meet state standards. State standards are used in the development of all of our products, so educators can be assured they meet the academic requirements of each state.

Common Core State Standards

Many lessons in this book are aligned to the Common Core State Standards (CCSS). The standards support the objectives presented throughout the lessons and are provided on the Digital Resource CD (standards.pdf).

McREL Compendium

We use the Mid-continent Research for Education and Learning (McREL) Compendium to create standards correlations. Each year, McREL analyzes state standards and revises the compendium. By following this procedure, McREL is able to produce a general compilation of national standards. Each lesson in this product is based on one or more McREL standards, which are provided on the Digital Resource CD (standards.pdf).

TESOL and WIDA Standards

The lessons in this book promote English language development for English language learners. The standards listed on the Digital Resource CD (standards.pdf) support the language objectives presented throughout the lessons.

Correlation to the Standards *(cont.)*

The main focus of the lessons presented in this book is to promote the integration of the arts in science. The standards for both the arts and science are provided on the Digital Resource CD (standards.pdf).

Common Core State Standards

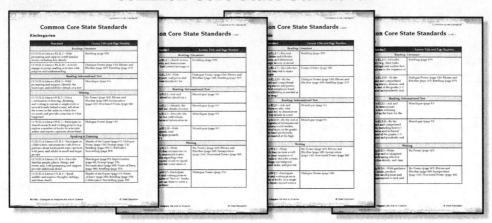

McREL Standards

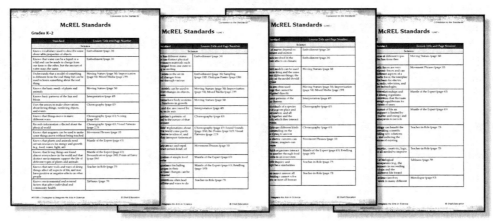

TESOL and WIDA Standards

Creative Movement

#51086—*Strategies to Integrate the Arts in Science*

Creative Movement

Understanding Creative Movement

Integrating creative movement across the curriculum is an engaging approach to learning that allows students to experience, translate, and communicate scientific ideas kinesthetically. In 1983, Howard Gardner identified bodily-kinesthetic intelligence within his theory of multiple intelligences (2011) as one way that students learn. Neuroscientists are finding that memory and recall is improved when the body is engaged in the learning process (Zull 2002) and that the mind uses the body to make sense of ideas (Carpenter 2010).

While important for all learners, opportunities to express themselves nonverbally can be particularly powerful for some students. Such opportunities can provide students with access to scientific content that would not be possible otherwise. Stacey Skoning (2008) states that creative movement, or dance, "is important to incorporate into our inclusive classrooms if we want to meet the needs of more diverse groups of students" (9).

Creative movement allows students to be physically active, which often increases students' attention span, but it is much more than just the incorporation of movement into classroom activities. When students are involved in creative movement, they become more mindful of their bodies' ability to communicate, explore what happens when they move with intention, engage in problem solving through movement, and develop awareness of their creative choices. It is important to keep the possibilities for this work in mind as your students explore these lessons.

As students deconstruct and reconstruct concepts, they take ownership of the ideas through kinesthetic means and creative choices. As choreographer and former elementary teacher Paula Aarons notes, "figuring out things in your body and through movement weaves ideas together. This builds a sense of intuitive knowledge, of working with an interchange of acting and responding, of physical problem solving" (Aarons, pers. comm. 2012).

Creative Movement (cont.)

Strategies for Creative Movement

✍ Embodiment

In this strategy, students use shapes (body shapes, lines, angles, curves), level (low, middle, high), and movement or gesture to *embody*, or show with their bodies, their understanding of concepts and terms. The strategy can be used to model complex ideas, helping students to grasp, investigate, and internalize concepts. Students can also create spontaneous creative movement to help them summarize or review their learning.

Working with others to embody ideas in movement can prompt students to discuss characteristics of a particular concept, both as they translate ideas into movement and also while they view the presentation of other groups' ideas. Dance artist Celeste Miller (Miller, pers. comm. 2012) suggests that the language of movement can provide a "palette for expression of both abstract and tangible ideas and see how different movement interpretations can convey the same ideas. Coming up with more than one approach for depicting an idea encourages creative and critical thinking. This strategy can help students solidify tangible ideas." Having groups of students embody the same concept allows them to see how different movement interpretations can convey the same ideas. Coming up with more than one approach for depicting an idea encourages creative and critical thinking. This strategy can help students solidify ideas and help you assess students' depth of understanding.

✍ Moving Statues

This strategy combines held poses with movement as students incorporate the use of shape (body shapes, lines, angles, curves), level (low, medium, high), and quality of movement (characteristics such as sustained, swing, percussive, collapsed), allowing them to make nuanced changes in moves. In moving statues, students begin from a still position in a particular shape and then initiate purposeful movement, which can help them look at both positioning as statues hold their form and how things shift when statues move. In science, this allows students to investigate phenomena that are not easily observable as the statues can serve as models for abstract concepts. Students can form moving statues alone, in pairs, or in groups.

A group statue results in a large fluid representation of a concept as students create an evolving model of the idea being explored. Moving statues can also require students to position themselves in relation to others. Through such experiences, creative movement can improve self-esteem and social functioning in addition to deepening understanding of science content (Theodorakou and Zervas 2003).

Creative Movement (cont.)

Interpretation

In this strategy, students explore and interpret physical, biological, or chemical actions and processes through abstract movement that symbolizes these processes. As movements are explored, students embody physical motions, qualities of forces, and directions of energy. Students explore and interpret a variety of physical states, qualities of motion, and changes over time. They interpret movements affected by the many modes of energy.

Choreography

Audiences can be mesmerized by dancers moving across the stage alone, in pairs, or in groups. Dancers seem to move seamlessly from individual locations as they join as a group and then part to return to individual spots. Choreographers orchestrate this motion through the planning and notation of movement.

Choreography requires students to decide how to incorporate movements, pathways, tempo, and location into a creative movement piece and then to notate or communicate those decisions. Without such notation, dance instructions could not be transmitted over time (Waters and Gibbons 2004).

Movement Phrases

In this strategy, students create a series of movements to represent the parts of a process or concept. They perform this series of movements, linking each to the next, to illustrate a series of steps or components within a curricular concept. When students link ideas, they can better understand relationships among concepts and form generalizations. As students create and build upon their movement ideas, they also develop the vocabulary of movement such as directional words (pathways) and levels (high, medium, low). According to Stacey Skoning (2008), "having a common movement vocabulary in the classroom benefits everyone because the common vocabulary makes it easier to discuss the movement phrases that are being created" (6).

Embodiment

Model Lesson: States of Matter

Model Lesson Overview

In this strategy, students use embodied movement to become water molecules and move in different ways to represent each state of matter. A simple narrative prompts students to move from one phase to another so that they represent all the states as well as the transitions.

Standards

K-2

- Knows vocabulary used to describe some observable properties of objects

- Knows that water can be a liquid or a solid and can be made to change from one form to the other, but the amount of water stays the same

- Improvises dances based on personal ideas and concepts from other sources

3-5

- Knows that matter has different states and that each state has distinct physical properties; some common materials such as water can be changed from one state to another by heating or cooling

- Knows that water exists in the air in different forms and changes from one form to another through various processes

- Knows how improvisation is used to discover and invent movement and to solve movement problems

6-8

- Knows that states of matter depend on molecular arrangement and motion

- Knows the processes involved in the water cycle and their effects on climatic patterns

- Understands how movement choices are used to communicate abstract ideas and themes in dance

Materials

- Images, videos, and articles about states of matter

- *Embodied Movement Planning Guide* (page 30, embodiedguide.pdf)

- *Six Qualities of Movement Reference Sheet* (pages 31–32, sixqualities.pdf)

- *Phase Change Narrative* (page 33, phasechange.pdf)

Embodiment *(cont.)*

Preparation

Read through *Phase Change Narrative* (page 33). Browse the library or the Internet for articles, images, and video clips to share with students about how molecules move. The Canadian Museum of Nature has a video about water molecules in various states that is under two minutes long (see the Recommended Resources in Appendix C). Additional suggestions are provided in the Specific Grade Level Ideas.

Procedure

1. Ask students to tell you what they know about states of matter in general, about the states of water and how it changes forms, and about sources of energy that affect states of matter. Show them images or examples of water in various states as you provide an explanation about how molecules change through each state. Share a short video that shows how molecules move in each state of matter and ask students to imagine that they are those molecules. Ask students to describe what they think moving like that would feel like.

2. Explain to students that they will embody, or show through movement, water molecules as they transform from one state to another. Divide students in groups of three to create water molecules—one student will be hydrogen and two students will be oxygen.

3. Distribute the *Embodied Movement Planning Guide* (page 30) activity sheet to students. Ask students to talk with their group about what happens to a water molecule as it moves from one state of matter to another and brainstorm movements they could use to embody each state of matter and its phase changes. If desired, distribute the *Six Qualities of Movement Reference Sheet* (pages 31–32) to students to use as a resource for movement ideas.

4. Explain to students that you will tell them a short narrative about water molecules moving together as they transform from one state of matter to another. Read from the *Phase Change Narrative* (page 33) activity sheet. Students will embody the water molecules as you narrate.

5. Ask students to stand together with their water molecule group. Read Part A of the narrative and have students move around the room to embody the water molecules. Before moving on to Part B, discuss with students what was happening to the molecules and ask them to use their scientific knowledge to help them predict what may happen next.

6. Read Part B of the narrative and have students continue to embody the molecules. Tell them that when the narrative says "some molecules," they will each decide if they will be part of that group. Stop again at the end of Part B when the water molecules have made it to a mountaintop in the form of a cloud. Discuss the concept of evaporation with students.

Embodiment *(cont.)*

7. Read Part C of the narrative and have students embody the molecules. Discuss the concept of condensation as molecules return to the ocean. As appropriate for your grade level, read Part D and Part E of the narrative, and have students embody water molecules during deposition and sublimation. Challenge students to integrate qualities from the *Six Qualities of Movement Reference Sheet* to show the kinds of movement molecules might make.

8. Have students develop new situations when water shifts from one phase to another, and have students move fluidly from one state of matter to the next without stopping for discussion. Ask students to consider how this becomes a molecule "dance" that can go on indefinitely as various molecules move to different areas with different energy input, similar to how water has been moving and transforming in and around the earth for millennia.

9. Use the Questions for Discussion to debrief and review.

Questions for Discussion

- What came up in your discussion about how to translate a scientific idea into movement?

- What science did you need to know about your molecule and its specific circumstances in order to translate it into movement?

- What choices did you make in your embodied representation?

- What struck you about how space was used as all students embodied the various states of matter?

- What scientific ideas were demonstrated?

Specific Grade Level Ideas

K–2

Students can focus on their senses to consider what the states of matter look and feel like. For example, have them consider how the hard texture of ice is different from the fluid texture of water. Have students embody the properties they notice, such as the hardness, the fluidity, and the weightless quality of water vapor rising into the air.

Students could also embody how other living things grow and change form, such as humans, animals, or plants.

Embodiment *(cont.)*

3–5

As students use their bodies to represent the molecules in each state of matter, they can also develop movements that carry them through the various seasons, showing different forms of precipitation (snow, hail, rain, etc.). While the focus of this lesson is on molecules and states of matter, it can also serve as an entry into the water cycle and related subjects.

Students could also embody the changes that happen in animals, such as metamorphosis, changes in organic matter as it decays, or changes in soil or in rocks.

6–8

Students can further develop narratives to embody various processes, such as percolation, and states of matter, such as plasma. They can expand the range and relationship of their movements to show the effect of these changes in matter on the water cycle and climatic patterns.

Students can also investigate the states of matter of multiple substances and develop their own movement narratives based on the scientific information about each specific element.

This strategy can help students investigate things that are not easily observable, such as chemicals, or consider things that interact with their environment and change, such as microorganisms.

Name _____ Date _____

Embodied Movement Planning Guide

Directions: Fill in the chart. Think about how molecules move in the different states of matter and phase changes. Describe how you will move to embody each state or phase change.

State of Matter	Movement Ideas
solid	
liquid	
gas	

Phase Change	Movement Ideas
freezing	
melting	
condensation	
vaporization	
sublimation	
deposition	

Six Qualities of Movement Reference Sheet

Percussive:

Percussive movements are quick, forceful, and sudden. They are broken up by quick pauses. Think of someone suddenly stomping his or her feet and pausing briefly afterward to increase the impact of the movement.

Sustained:

Sustained movements are flowing, ongoing, and smooth. Think of sliding your foot out away from your body in a long, fluid push.

Vibratory:

Vibratory movements are similar to percussive ones, but they are quicker and less forceful. The movements could involve tapping or shaking.

Six Qualities of Movement Reference Sheet *(cont.)*

Suspension:

A suspension movement is the slight pause that occurs between motions. The pause can draw attention to the movement just before or after.

Collapse:

Collapse movements give in to the pull of gravity. They can be sudden movements, such as a quick fall to the floor, or they can be gradual motions, such as the controlled lowering of your leg.

Swing/Pendular:

A swing or pendular movement goes back and forth. An example would be an arm that swings up high, pauses briefly, and then returns back down.

Phase Change Narrative

Teacher Directions: Read the following narrative aloud to students in order to contextualize and guide their movement as water molecules.

Part A: Melting

A long time ago, water molecules existed in a glacier. All around them was ice— huge mountains of ice. They were all so close together and could move so little that it looked as if they were standing still. After many, many centuries, the molecules, warmed by the sun, began to move. At first, they moved in slow motion…then faster. All around them the other molecules were moving, too. Soon, they were all moving along a riverbed. They rushed along together until they arrived at a huge body of water, such as a lake or ocean.

Part B: Evaporation

Soon, all the water molecules were traveling in different directions around the globe, dispersed in different ocean currents. Some molecules traveled to cool climates and cool water, and others traveled to warmer water. In the warmer water, the molecules that were near the surface got so warm that they left the ocean waters and drifted up into the sky, forming beautiful white clouds. The warm breezes over the ocean then carried them long distances until they came across the land. Over the land they noticed streams and rivers below and the mountains nearby. Many clouds traveled over the mountains with the wind.

Part C: Precipitation

One of the clouds got bigger with water molecules until all at once they clung closely to one another and formed water droplets that started to fall from the sky down to the land. These droplets fell on the earth and ran together across the hills until they found a river. As they joined the river, they went over the rocks as the river ran quickly down the mountain. Finally, they all arrived at the ocean.

Part D: Deposition

Another cloud full of water molecules went North in the wintertime. It was freezing up there and the water vapor quickly transformed into icy snow that blanketed the cold earth below.

Part E: Sublimation

The earth was blanketed with snow. The next day, warm weather came and the molecules on top jumped right up into the warm air, creating fog as they sublimated from solid to vapor.

Moving Statues

Model Lesson: Scientific Models

Model Lesson Overview

In this strategy, students create a model to represent a complex scientific process that is difficult to see with the naked eye. Students view and compare various models of photosynthesis. Then, they create a frozen scene by forming parts of plants and elements with their bodies. Finally, they move together to model the process of photosynthesis.

Standards

K–2

- Understands that a model of something is different from the real thing but can be used to learn something about the real thing

- Knows the basic needs of plants and animals

- Knows how dance is different from other forms of human movement

3–5

- Understands that models can be used to represent and predict changes in objects, events, and processes

- Knows that organisms have body systems that serve specific functions in growth

- Knows how a variety of solutions can be used to solve a given movement problem

6–8

- Knows that different models can be used to represent the same thing and the same model can represent different things; the kind and complexity of the model should depend on its purpose

- Knows that models are often used to think about things that cannot be observed or investigated directly

- Understands the importance of movement initiation

9–12

- Knows the structures of different types of cell parts and the functions they perform

- Understands how movement choices are used to communicate abstract ideas in dance

Materials

- Multiple models of photosynthesis

- *Moving Statue Documentation Form* (page 39, movingstatue.pdf)

Moving Statues *(cont.)*

Preparation

Find as many models as you can that represent photosynthesis. These can be illustrations, computer graphics, videos, or three-dimensional models. Look for multiple models that represent photosynthesis in different ways to help students see that a single concept can be represented in any number of ways. Try to find images that include different kinds of plants and present different symbols for each element and each part of the process, including the byproduct. Additional suggestions are provided in the Specific Grade Level Ideas.

Procedure

1. Ask students to tell you what they know about photosynthesis and record their ideas for them to reference throughout the lesson.

2. Ask students to imagine they can just stand in the sun and the rain and breathe and let their bodies create their food without having to find food or cook it. As appropriate to your grade level, explain the process of photosynthesis and have students imagine what they would experience (as a plant) during each step in the process.

3. Show students a model of photosynthesis and ask them to describe what they see. What do they notice about shapes of the plants and the location of each element? Show several varied models of photosynthesis and discuss with students the similarities and differences between the models. Discuss the purpose of scientific models as a way to represent information that is difficult or impractical to observe in real life.

4. Explain to students that they will be creating models for photosynthesis by using their own bodies as "moving statues." Explain that they will create a frozen scene by forming a part of a plant or an element with their bodies. Then, they will move together to show the process of photosynthesis.

5. Divide students into groups of eight and provide each group with multiple images of photosynthesis. Distribute the *Moving Statue Documentation Form* (page 39) activity sheet to each group. Ask students to choose one plant part or element from the first column to model with their bodies. Tell students to consider how they will represent their plant part or element by making shapes with their bodies as they plan their statues. Have them describe these body shapes in the chart.

6. Have students discuss and plan their individual locations within the statue, as well as how each group member will move in relation to the others to show the process of photosynthesis. Ask students to record this information on their chart.

Moving Statues *(cont.)*

7. Provide students time to rehearse and revise their moving statues. Use the Planning Questions to guide students. Remind them to begin in stillness and then transition slowly to movement.

8. Have each group present its moving statue to the class. Use the Questions for Discussion to debrief.

Planning Questions

- How will you position yourselves at the beginning to show the parts of your model?

- Will you begin your movement all together or one at a time?

- How will you move individually and in relation to each other to model photosynthesis?

- When and how will you end your movement and return to a frozen position?

Questions for Discussion

- What did it feel like to try representing a particular concept?

- What did you find most challenging? Why?

- How did movement help you understand abstract concepts?

- How did you use movement to show particular processes?

- How can you make a dance representing a scientific model?

- How do you think models can serve scientific inquiry?

Moving Statues *(cont.)*

Specific Grade Level Ideas

K–2

With younger students, help student volunteers create a model of a moving statue for the class so they can see the process. Keep the model simple enough for students to understand. To help students understand the strategy, compare the process of moving statues to freeze dancing in reverse. Students start frozen and then begin to move slowly in very purposeful and particular ways, thinking about the concepts they are representing.

This strategy can be used to represent other processes, such as plant or animal growth and transformation, as well as interactions within systems, such as the human body.

3–5

Have students begin by representing the body system of plants to show the specific functions of its various parts and then explore photosynthesis. Have students investigate how plants may react to particular changes in their environment, such as darkness, lack of water, or extreme temperatures. Once students understand these concepts, they can move their statues in new ways to represent the various scenarios.

As an extension, this strategy can also be used to investigate various systems in the human body, such as the cardiovascular system or the respiratory system.

Moving Statues (cont.)

6–8

Students can focus on both macro and micro levels to understand the intricacies of photosynthesis and respiration. Have students create a model of the global carbon cycle by combining the various models of photosynthesis and respiration into an ecosystem. They can investigate technologies that release CO_2 and see what happens to the carbon cycle. They can use the model to understand what happens as well as to predict what may happen with any number of environmental impacts.

Students can use this strategy to model any set of interactions that are difficult to see with the naked eye, ranging from biological to chemical interactions, such as cell division or crystallization.

9–12

Students can investigate respiration at the cellular level. As an extension, they can create models with their bodies for aerobic and anaerobic respiration.

This strategy can also be used to investigate the relationship within and between organs in the respiratory system and other systems in the body, such as the cardiovascular system, nervous system, and others. Each of these can be investigated separately through moving statues or in relation to each other. Students can look at respiration, decay, cellular growth, and division as well as relationships among cells and molecules.

Name _____   Date _____

Moving Statue Documentation Form

Directions: Embody each item by imagining you are that item. Then, fill in the chart.

Group members: _____

Item	Shape What shape might you make with your body?	Function What function do you play in photosynthesis?	Location Where will you place yourself in relation to the others in your group?	Movement How will you move to represent your part in the process of photosynthesis?
leaf				
stem				
roots				
fruit				
sunlight				
water				
carbon dioxide				
oxygen				

Interpretation

Model Lesson: Rotation and Revolution

Model Lesson Overview

In this strategy, students interpret movements to physically discover and authentically learn the physical principles of rotation and revolution by relating them to movements in the solar system. Students often confuse rotation and revolution, and this model lesson provides an engaging exploration that will help students understand and retain these concepts.

Standards

K-2

- Knows basic patterns of the Sun and Moon
- Moves his or her body in a variety of controlled ways
- Creates shapes at low, middle, and high levels

3-5

- Knows that night and day are caused by the Earth's rotation on its axis
- Knows how ideas are communicated through movement elements
- Knows basic actions and movement elements and how they communicate ideas

6-8

- Knows the movement patterns of the planets in our Solar System
- Understands various movements and their underlying principles
- Understands the action and movement elements observed in dance, and knows appropriate movement/dance vocabulary

Materials

- Reference materials on the planets (or student Internet access)
- *Solar System Model 1* (solarsystem1.pdf) or *Solar System Model 2* (solarsystem2.pdf)
- Music that connotes outer space
- *Planetary Movement* (page 44, planetary.pdf)

Interpretation *(cont.)*

Preparation

Gather reference materials on the planets or prepare for students to access the Internet to conduct research. Refer to *Solar System Model 1* (solarsystem1.pdf) or *Solar System Model 2* (solarsystem2.pdf) on the Digital Resource CD for solar system models to share with students. Find a space large enough for students to explore the concept of the solar system through movement. Prepare to play music, such as Gustav Holtz's *The Planets*, or other music that connotes outer space. Additional suggestions are provided in the Specific Grade Level Ideas.

Procedure

1. With students, brainstorm and record a list of movement verbs for students to reference throughout the lesson, such as *wave, jump, glide, rotate, revolve, turn*, and *twist*. Discuss the differences between the movements, focusing the discussion on the difference between *rotation* and *revolution*.

2. Invite students to an open area. As a warm-up activity, have students demonstrate each verb from the list with their bodies several times. After this exploration, ask students to rotate, first in one place, and then while moving slowly around the room.

3. Divide students into groups of 4 or 5. Have one student in each group stand in the center of the group with the other students forming a circle around him or her about two feet away. Ask students to rotate in place, including the student in the center. Then, ask them to stop rotating and to begin slowly revolving around the student in the center, first in one direction and then in the other. Then, have students rotate while performing another movement, such as *glide*, varying the verb so that students can *jump, hop, skip*, or *tiptoe* as they revolve. Finally, ask them to slowly and carefully rotate and revolve at the same time.

4. Have each group choose a planet from the solar system to represent. Have students use reference materials or the Internet to investigate how many moons their planet has and how far it is from the sun. If necessary, regroup some students or invent moons for planets with few or no moons.

5. Provide space for students to use their bodies to interpret what they learned about the motion of their planet and its moons. Ask students in each group to take turns as the planet and its moons as they practice revolving and rotating. Students representing Saturn can hold out their arms or use colored silks to create the rings.

Interpretation *(cont.)*

6. Select one student, or several students standing closely together, to represent the sun. Place the planet groups at appropriate distances around the sun, using the *Solar System Model 1* (solarsystem1.pdf) or *Solar System Model 2* (solarsystem2.pdf) sheet on the Digital Resource CD for reference. Have all the groups revolve around the sun together at the same velocity. Have students representing planets stop rotating so the moons revolve around the rotating planets alone. Then, have the planets carefully revolve around the sun while the moons are revolving around the planets. They must move slowly!

7. Allow students to improvise and experiment with rotation and revolution as you play music for them.

8. Have students record their thinking on the *Planetary Movement* (page 44) activity sheet.

9. Debrief with students, using the Questions for Discussion.

Questions for Discussion

- What is the difference between *rotate* and *revolve*?

- How does Earth move around the sun? Does it rotate, revolve, or both?

- How do the other planets move around the sun?

- How many moons does each planet have?

- What is the closest planet to the sun? The farthest?

- How would you describe your improvisation?

Interpretation *(cont.)*

Specific Grade Level Ideas

K–2

Have students interpret the movements of Earth, the moon, and the sun without including the other planets. Other potential interpretations include exploring how weather is affected by the tilt of Earth on its axis in relation to where Earth is in its 365 $\frac{1}{4}$ days of travel around the sun. This strategy can be used to explore other science concepts regarding movements, such as waves and cloud formation or animal locomotion.

3–5

Students can explore the activity as written to formalize their understanding of the relationships and movements of the bodies in the solar system. Have students investigate the changes in shadows during the course of the day and make connections between rotation and revolution. This strategy can be used to investigate the movement of other natural elements, such as rhizomatic plant growth or wind and water.

6–8

Students can investigate a lunar and solar eclipse, the cause of seasons, and the number and type of artificial satellites around Earth and interpret the movement of satellites as they revolve around Earth. They can also develop parameters about other movement phenomena as well, such as ocean and river currents.

Name _____   Date _____

Planetary Movement

Directions: Write or draw your answers in the boxes.

What planet did you interpret in your movement? Draw it with its moons.	Use movement words to describe how your moons move around the planet.
Make a sketch to show the relationship of your planet to the sun.	Draw your planet and the sun with arrows to show the rotation and revolution movements.

Choreography

Model Lesson: Bird Migration

Model Lesson Overview

In this lesson, students develop choreography that represents birds' migration to and from their wintering homes. Through careful observation and notation, students use their bodies to investigate the pathways, movements, and tempo of birds migrating, and transform and communicate their learning into a choreographed dance.

Standards

K–2

- Uses the senses to make observations about living things, nonliving objects, and events

- Knows that things move in many different ways

- Records information collected about the physical world

- Creates a sequence with a beginning, middle, and ending

3–5

- Knows that an organism's patterns of behavior are related to the nature of that organism's environment

- Knows that scientists' explanations about what happens in the world come partly from what they observe (evidence), and partly from how they interpret (inference) their observations

- Creates and repeats a brief sequence of related movements that has a sense of rhythmic completion

6–8

- Knows that all individuals of a species that exist together at a given place and time make up a population, and all populations living together and the physical factors with which they interact compose an ecosystem

- Knows that scientists use different kinds of investigations, depending on the questions they are trying to answer

- Understands that the choreographic process of reordering involves separating specific movements or movement phrases from their original relationship and restructuring them in a different pattern

Choreography *(cont.)*

Materials

- Images and videos of local birds in the process of migration
- *Scientific Observation Notes* (page 49, scientificnotes.pdf)
- *Choreographic Notation Sheet* (page 50, notationsheet.pdf)
- Colored pencils

Preparation

Conduct research on birds that migrate to and from your area along with when the migration occurs. The Cornell Lab of Ornithology is a great web resource. This lesson is best taught when students can actually see birds migrating overhead in real life. If this is not possible, browse the Internet for images and videos of local birds in the process of migration for students to observe. Also, find an open space large enough for students to explore bird migration through movement. Additional suggestions are provided in the Specific Grade Level Ideas.

Procedure

1. Ask students to share what they know about birds in their area and if they notice birds feeding or flying nearby. Ask them to describe the birds with as much detail as possible. Do they fly alone or in groups? What do they look like when they fly? What and where have they noticed birds eating? Do they know if they migrate? If so, what do they know about their migration? Record details students remember for them to reference throughout the lesson, and identify the gaps.

2. Explain to students that they will be learning about local migratory birds through observation. Then, they will observe and document the qualities of the movements of individual birds and create choreography that shares the characteristics of this movement and tracks the migration of a population of birds.

3. If possible, invite students to look at the sky for migrating birds and identify the kinds of birds they spot. If locally observing birds is not possible, show students images and/or videos of a bird population you have identified from your area.

4. Distribute the *Scientific Observation Notes* (page 49) activity sheet and ask students to sketch the birds' behavior and placement, such as movements, flying formations, landing spaces, etc. Tell students they can use words, symbols, arrows, or lines to record what they see.

5. Divide students into groups of 5 or 6. Ask individual students to try capturing the characteristics of a bird's movement. Then, ask each group of students to try moving together as noted in their observations, imagining they are part of a flock. Encourage students to notice the spatial relationship to one another. How does each of their movements affect the other students' movements? Have students discuss what they notice.

Choreography *(cont.)*

6. Ask students to review their information and discuss the most noticeable movements and patterns, considering what kinds of movements (both individual and collective) they want to include in their choreography (flight formation, landing, eating, etc.).

7. Show students the space they will be using for their choreography, and ask them to establish where they will start and where they will "migrate." Have them consider both the beginning and ending environments as well as any stops along the way. Tell them to experiment by moving across that space, first individually, and then together as a group. Remind them to consider the flight formation from their observations.

8. Distribute the *Choreographic Notation Sheet* (page 50) activity sheet and colored pencils to each group. Tell students to decide on a sequence of movements that works and to note where each student will be. Have students use lines and arrows to note the path they will each be taking to cross the distance.

9. Ask students to rehearse and revise as needed. If needed, distribute a second copy of the *Choreographic Notation Sheet* activity sheet to each group for final notations. This recording should map the trajectory and movement of each member of the group in their final choreography.

10. Have each group perform their choreography for the class. Then, use the Questions for Discussion to debrief the activity.

Questions for Discussion

- How did embodying the movements of birds and moving in similar formations and patterns help you understand birds, their movements, and migrations?

- What did you notice when watching the choreography of other groups?

- How did moving like a bird make you aware of your own body and of spatial relationships with those around you?

- How does choreographing bird movements and migrations mirror human movements and interactions?

- How might choreography of human migration be similar to or different from your bird migration choreography?

- What can we learn about how birds flock, migrate, and nest by observing and notating their movements, position, and speed?

- What are the qualities of bird movement?

Choreography (cont.)

Specific Grade Level Ideas

K–2

Students can look at birds both in real life and in video clips to make general observations and movement with simple, short choreographed sequences. They can make drawings for their notations and a general line sketch of how they will move within a limited number of movements and pathways.

This strategy can also be used to investigate how other animals move in relation to each other, such as various animals in the ocean. Students can consider something as small as a coral reef or as big as the open ocean.

3–5

Students can reach a higher level of complexity about what they observe. Observations can include features of birds' trajectories, such as stops for feeding, and students can develop a choreography that includes multiple sequences from departure through their trajectory and their arrival at their wintering homes. They can include movement to show emotion and consider the particular elements of each location, such as heat and food availability.

This strategy can also be used to look at how other animals migrate, such as butterflies or whales. Students can investigate how other animals move and how they are equipped to function in particular ecosystems, such as the ocean, the desert, the forest, or the jungle.

6–8

Students can investigate the ecosystems that birds or other animals move through and consider the various factors that make birds move from one place to another as well as the animal behavior component of how they move as a group. Provide information on the ecosystems that support the particular population of animals you are investigating and ask questions to arrive at an understanding. What is the birds' habitat during the summer? Where are their wintering homes? Why do they travel? Students can investigate food sources, weather, nesting places, etc. They can also consider animals' effects on the ecosystem and consider endangered species, such as the Whooping Crane, to explore the impact of various environmental factors on the species.

Students can use this strategy to observe and investigate any group of moving things, such as the planets, cells, particles of matter, etc.

Name _____   Date _____

Scientific Observation Notes

Directions: As you observe birds' migratory movements, take notes using the chart.

Bird name:
How do the birds move their bodies? Wings? Heads? Feet?
Draw a picture or symbol to represent the path of the birds' movement.

Name _____   Date _____

Choreographic Notation Sheet

Directions: Use the space to map out the movement paths each student will take in the choreography as they migrate. Use a dot to indicate where each student begins and arrows of different colors to represent each path a student will take. Use the Key to indicate which color represents each student.

Key:

Student #1 name _____   Color: _____

Student #2 name _____   Color: _____

Student #3 name _____   Color: _____

Student #4 name _____   Color: _____

Student #5 name _____   Color: _____

Student #6 name _____   Color: _____

Movement Phrases

Model Lesson: Magnetic Transportation

Model Lesson Overview

In this lesson, students work in groups to create a series of sequential movements (movement phrases) to function as a transportation machine/system. Students are challenged to use various nonlocomotive movement qualities (swing, vibrate, glide, etc.) and movement levels (high, middle, low) to use magnetism to move a metal object from one student to the next until it reaches its destination.

Standards

K–2

- Knows that magnets can be used to make some things move without being touched

- Knows how a variety of solutions can be used to solve a given movement problem

- Uses basic nonlocomotor/axial movements

3–5

- Knows that magnets attract and repel each other and attract certain kinds of other materials

- Uses basic nonlocomotor/axial movements

- Uses kinesthetic awareness, concentration, and focus in performing movement skills

6–8

- Knows that just as electric currents can produce magnetic forces, magnets can cause electric currents

- Knows the critical elements that contribute to a dance in terms of space, time, and force/energy

9–12

- Knows that magnetic forces are very closely related to electric forces and can be thought of as different aspects of a single electromagnetic force; the interplay of these forces is the basis for electric motors, generators, radio, television, and many other modern technologies

- Uses appropriate skeletal alignment, body-part articulation, strength, flexibility, agility, and coordination in locomotor and nonlocomotor/axial movements

Movement Phrases *(cont.)*

Materials

- Assorted magnets

- Assorted small objects, including some made of aluminum, steel, and other metals

- *Magnet Experimentation Documentation* (page 56, magnet.pdf)

- *Nonlocomotive Movement Reference and Notation* (page 57, nonlocomotive.pdf)

Preparation

Gather an array of magnets of various sizes, shapes, and strengths. Gather objects for students to experiment with using the magnets. These should include small- to medium-sized metallic objects that magnets will attract and some that magnets will not attract. You can also invite students to bring small objects from home that they think may be attracted by magnets. Create a group of objects for each group of students that includes both kinds of objects. Each group should also have at least one magnet per student.

As inspiration for real-life applications of magnetic transportation technology, you may want to familiarize yourself with magnetic levitation transportation systems. Conduct an Internet search for "maglev transportation" using the search engine of your choice. If you want to provide a specific example, search for "maglev transportation in Tokyo" where this system is already in use. Additional suggestions are provided in the Specific Grade Level Ideas.

Procedure

1. Show students some magnets and ask them to share what they know about magnets. Ask them if they know any ways in which magnets are used. Share with them how magnets can be used to fill important needs, such as transportation via "maglev" trains.

2. Explain to students that they are going to experiment with creating a transportation machine using magnets that is powered by their bodies to transport objects. Divide students into groups of 4 or 5, and supply each group with magnets and objects to test. Distribute the *Magnet Experimentation Documentation* (page 56) activity sheet. Have each group work together to experiment with magnets and record their findings.

3. Ask students to each hold one magnet and try to pass the various objects from one student to the next using the magnets. Have students record their findings. Based on that information, have each group choose one object that they will use for their magnetic transportation movement phrase.

Movement Phrases *(cont.)*

4. Distribute the *Nonlocomotive Movement Reference and Notation* (page 57) activity sheet and review it with students. Explain nonlocomotive movement, which is moving in place without going anywhere.

5. Ask each group of students to stand and line up with enough space so that when students stretch out their arms, they can touch each other's hands. Have students practice each of the nonlocomotive movements in the chart by calling out a movement and a level for students to perform, such as "high, twist," or "middle, swing."

6. Ask the first student in each group to perform one of the movements and complete it by touching the hand of the next student, "passing" the movement on. The next student should do another nonlocomotive movement and touch the next student, and so on. Explain that each student is a part in the machine, creating a movement phrase. They each represent one part of a transportation machine.

7. Ask students to hold a magnet. Tell the first student in each line to hold the group's selected object. Challenge students to transport their selected object from one end of their transportation machine to the other, using a nonlocomotive movement phrase. Each student will make one movement and pass the object to the next student to get the object to the other end of the line. Specify that each group's machine is to include at least three nonlocomotive movements and all three levels. Students can note their movement selections on the *Nonlocomotive Movement Reference and Notation* activity sheet.

8. Ask students to experiment with some variations and decide on their final movement phrase.

9. Have each group show their movement phrase to the class as they transport their selected object. Compare the distances each group's object traveled and use the Questions for Discussion to debrief.

Questions for Discussion

- What movements did you choose to move your object with and why?

- What did you observe about how far you could move the object without locomotive movement?

- What did you observe about the various movements other groups used to move their object forward?

- What did you find most challenging? Why?

Movement Phrases *(cont.)*

Specific Grade Level Ideas

K–2

Have students play and experiment with magnets and ask them questions about what they notice. You can facilitate the activity as a whole class by having students stand in a circle as they explore nonlocomotive movement and then use magnets to move a metal object around the circle. They can experiment with various movements to get the object to go all the way around.

Students could also use movement phrases to represent other things that travel across space, such as waves in the ocean.

3–5

Students can work in small groups and repeat their movement phrases as they transport multiple objects, challenging them to move their objects as steadily as possible or moving multiple objects at the same time. They will need to use concentration and focus to repeat their movements at the right tempo so the object travels smoothly without dropping or stopping.

You can also use this activity to investigate gravity by using other kinds of objects such as small balls. Students can create movement phrases to represent other kinds of systems, such as how a grape gets from a vine to their homes or a seed going from pod to a place where it can grow.

6–8

Challenge students to investigate the relationship between electric currents and magnets. Because the direction of the electrical fields that are produced by an electrical current are perpendicular to the direction of the current flow, students will need to combine two different movements. When a student moves in an opposite direction, the rotating or revolving students also change direction. A piece of music with a slow beat to accompany these movements will allow students to flow and glide smoothly in both directions.

Students could also create movement phrases to represent traveling sound waves or light waves and take into consideration other variables, such as pitch.

Movement Phrases *(cont.)*

9–12

Have students do a more in-depth investigation of real-life applications of magnetic forces, such as transportation systems that use magnetic levitation to propel vehicles. In this case, the work can also cross over to engineering and to human impact on the environment as they consider the efficiency of magnetic levitation with no friction and less energy from fossil fuels. Students could use their movement phrases to investigate maglev transportation systems and other concepts, such as circuits and conduction.

Name _____ Date _____

Magnet Experimentation Documentation

Directions: List the items that are and are not attracted to magnets. Then, answer the questions.

Attracted to Magnets	Not Attracted to Magnets

1. What do you notice about the objects that are attracted to magnets? What do they have in common?

   _____

   _____

2. Use various magnets to experiment with picking up and passing objects from magnet to magnet. Note which magnet works best with which object.

   _____

   _____

3. What object can most easily be picked up and passed around by all the magnets in your group?

   _____

   _____

Name _____   Date _____

Nonlocomotive Movement Reference and Notation

Directions: Use at least three of the following nonlocomotive movements in your movement phrase. Use all three levels. Record each student's movement and level. Consider what kind of machine part you may be in the process of transportation.

Nonlocomotor Movements   **Levels**

twisting   turning   low

bending   swinging   middle

swaying   gliding   high

stretching

Record the movement each student will be performing:

Student #1: _____

Movement: _____ Level: _____

Student #2: _____

Movement: _____ Level: _____

Student #3: _____

Movement: _____ Level: _____

Student #4: _____

Movement: _____ Level: _____

Student #5: _____

Movement: _____ Level: _____

#51086—*Strategies to Integrate the Arts in Science*

Drama

#51086—Strategies to Integrate the Arts in Science

Drama

Understanding Drama

Integrating drama into the science classroom can deepen students' connection with science concepts and foster students' ability to find relevance to their own lives and interests. Drama can provide engaging contexts for exploring scientific ideas. By enacting scenes that connect to a scientific concept or skill, students can apply their learning in real-world settings.

When we integrate drama into the science classroom, we invite our students to consider particular situations in which scientific ideas are embedded. As students explore these scenarios, they uncover and deepen their scientific thinking, make personal connections to the sciences, and recognize its real-world relevance. Christopher Andersen (2004) notes that drama has the ability to recreate the essential elements in the world; as such, drama can place the sciences in authentic situations that make sense to students.

When students explore the sciences through the lens of a character, they are called upon to imagine themselves working through processes, events, and dilemmas. In their roles, they must make choices, solve problems, translate concepts, and articulate ideas. This process requires students to explain, persuade, clarify, and negotiate their thinking (Elliott-Johns et al. 2012). As students investigate perspectives that are different from their own, they expand their worldviews and develop an awareness of their own. Such experiences help students clarify their thinking, understand different perspectives, and consider new strategies for solving problems.

Drama will provide your students with contexts that can ground their scientific investigations. These drama strategies provide a rich context for scientific investigations where students imagine themselves in a variety of science-related situations. Embedding scientific ideas into dramatic scenarios motivates students to participate eagerly in the exploration of ideas from multiple perspectives.

Drama (cont.)

Strategies for Drama

Mantle of the Expert

Developed by dramatist Dorothy Heathcote, this strategy asks students to imagine that they have a particular expertise that informs how they approach the work and how they present their ideas. Inviting students to imagine that they have a specific frame of reference can be a catalyst that deepens their interest and sense of authority in an area of study. Heathcote and Bolton (1995) note, "Thinking from within a situation immediately forces a different kind of thinking. Research has convincingly shown that the determining factor in children's ability to perform particular intellectual tasks is the context in which the task is embedded. In mantle of the expert, problems and challenges arise within a context that makes them both motivating and comprehensible" (viii).

When students are in a dramatic role, they begin to think through the lens of the character they are playing, developing the attitude and ways of thinking of a scientific expert. Being asked questions about the decisions they make in role, called "hot-seating," can draw evidence of students' scientific thinking.

Teacher-in-Role

In process drama, the teacher and students work together to explore a problem or situation in an unscripted manner through improvisation (O'Neill 1995). In this strategy, the teacher takes on the role of a character to introduce a drama. Teachers can model the kind of work that they will ask students to do or set the stage for a dramatic scene. Either way, the strategy serves as an invitation for students to join in the dramatic work, to imagine, or to consider *what if?* There are a variety of ways that the teacher can create this role. For example, the teacher can portray a scientist in a book who presents his or her predictions and research, become a historical figure in engineering who shares thoughts on possible designs that would impact an environmental issue that would have significant impact on future events, or introduce an investigation by depicting an artist who shares the details of an observation and asks others to participate as related characters. The allure of seeing their teacher willing to engage in the creation of a scene compels students to suspend their disbelief and join in the dramatic enactment.

Drama (cont.)

∞ Tableaux

Sometimes called image theater or human sculpture, *tableau* is a French word meaning "frozen picture." It is a drama technique that allows for the exploration of an idea without movement or speaking. In this strategy, students use their bodies to create a shape or full picture to tell a story, represent a concept literally, or create a tangible representation of an abstract concept. Working with physical stance (low, medium, high), suggested relationships (body placement and eye contact), and a sense of action frozen in time allows students to explore ideas and provides a range of ways for students to share what they know about a concept. One student can create a frozen image or a group can work together to create an image. The process of creating group tableaux prompts discussion of the characteristics of what is being portrayed. The learning occurs in the process of translating ideas to physical representation. Tableaux can also be used as a way to gain entry into a complex idea or bigger project (Walker, Tabone, and Weltsek 2011).

∞ Monologue

A *monologue* is a dramatic scene performed by one person. In creating a monologue, students take on the perspective of a character in a story, real or imagined, and speak directly to the audience for one to three minutes. The character must be established without interactions with others (that would be a dialogue) and must speak in a way that engages the audience with this singular focus.

There are often monologues in stories and plays that illuminate what a character is thinking. Most often, a monologue reveals a conflict of some kind that the character is wrestling with, a choice to be made, or a problem to be solved. Note that variations include *soliloquy* in which a character is speaking to him or herself. The creation of a monologue provides the opportunity to investigate what Barry Lane calls a "thoughtshot" of a character's inner thinking (1992).

This strategy allows students to "get into the head" of a particular character. Eventually, the goal is for students to create their own monologues, but you may want to introduce the strategy by having students explore prepared ones in resources such as *Magnificent Monologues for Kids 2* by Chambers Stevens and *Minute Monologues for Kids* by Ruth Mae Roddy. Then, students can develop characters and create and perform monologues for inanimate objects or forces, or students can portray specific characters (a historical figure, a character from a book, a newspaper article, a painting, or they can create an imagined character). In order for a monologue to be dramatic, the character must have some tension or conflict that he or she is wrestling with. This conflict can be an internal or external dilemma. Its resolution or the naming of it will create dramatic interest.

Drama (cont.)

Improvisation

A foundation of drama, *improvisation* is when individuals create a scene or dramatization "in the moment," making it up as they go. This kind of drama unfolds in exciting and often unpredictable ways as circumstances and character motivation come together to influence how a scene progresses. Improvisation can develop divergent thinking, language use, and social skills while allowing students to test ideas in a situation that is safe but feels real.

Mantle of the Expert

Model Lesson: Zoo Design

Model Lesson Overview

In this strategy, students problem-solve in the role of a zoo exhibit designer, present their ideas, and, to probe each group's vision further, they answer questions about their design asked by fellow classmates who are acting as zoo administrators, animal behaviorists, and wildlife educators.

Standards

K-2

- Knows that plants and animals need certain resources for energy and growth (e.g., food, water, light, air)

- Knows that living things are found almost everywhere in the world and that distinct environments support the life of different types of plants and animals

- Engages in both fantasy dramatic play and dramatic play that is based on real experiences

3-5

- Knows the organization of simple food chains and food webs

- Knows that all organisms (including humans) cause changes in their environments, and these changes can be beneficial or detrimental

- Assumes roles that exhibit concentration and contribute to the action of dramatizations based on personal experience and heritage, imagination, literature, and history

6-8

- Knows ways in which organisms interact and depend on one another through food chains and food webs in an ecosystem

- Understands how descriptions, dialogue, and actions are used to discover, articulate, and justify character motivation

- Invents character behaviors based on the observation of interactions, ethical choices, and emotional responses of people

9-12

- Knows how the interrelationships and interdependencies among organisms generate stable ecosystems that fluctuate around a state of rough equilibrium for hundreds or thousands of years

- Knows how the amount of life an environment can support is limited by the availability of matter and energy and the ability of the ecosystem to recycle materials

- Develops, communicates, and sustains characters that communicate with audiences in improvisations and informal or formal productions

Mantle of the Expert *(cont.)*

Materials

- Books, images, videos, or other materials about animal habitats and ecosystems

- *Zoo Director Memo* (page 70, zoomemo.pdf)

- *Brainstorming Guide* (page 71, brainstormingguide.pdf)

- *Presentation Guide* (page 72, presentationguide.pdf)

Preparation

Identify a diverse array of exhibit themes that you would like student groups to work on, and locate books, images, videos, and other information related to each. Students will explore a diverse array of habitats (e.g., desert, ocean, river, jungle), animal types (e.g., dolphin, gorilla, snake, spider), or a collection of animals across one habitat (e.g., see the elephant exhibit at the San Diego Zoo, which includes elephants, lions, secretary birds, dung beetles, rattlesnakes, and California condors) that are all interconnected. If time allows, visit zoo exhibits in person or online to give students ideas about how to best proceed.

Read the *Zoo Director Memo* (page 70) activity sheet and decide if you will use it as written or adapt it to meet the needs of your students.

Determine how you will group students as they create plans for zoo habitats. Groups of 3 or 4 are suggested. Give at least two groups the same animal or concept, which will serve to show how an engineering design can be approached from different perspectives. Sharing a similar focus also deepens the knowledge of the group in a particular area so that when students are watching other presentations, they will be able to ask in-depth questions of the panels. Additional suggestions are provided in the Specific Grade Level Ideas.

Procedure

1. Have students think of times they have been to a zoo or an aquarium and noticed the animals living in habitats that have been designed to mimic the animals' natural habitat in the wild. What kinds of habitats did they see, and what kind of animal behaviors do they remember?

2. Invite students to imagine that they work at a zoo and that they have been asked to replicate the natural habitat of one of the animals. Explain that their role will consist of brainstorming ideas for new animal exhibits that will provide an enjoyable habitat for the animal while also educating the public about the species, often referred to as *animal enrichment*.

Mantle of the Expert *(cont.)*

3. Tell students that animal enrichment is when a space is designed to promote natural behavior and offer many choices that stimulate interest and exploration to enhance the life and well being of the species. Tell students that they will receive a memo from the director of the zoo explaining their next exhibit design assignment.

4. Divide students into small groups. Assign an animal to each group. Distribute the *Zoo Director Memo* (page 70) activity sheet to each group. Have students read the memo and discuss the animal they have been assigned.

5. Distribute the *Brainstorming Guide* (page 71) activity sheet and have students complete it with their groups.

6. Check in with groups as they are working to hear their preliminary ideas, to help shape their design concepts for the exhibit, and to prompt them to consider how to present their design ideas. Use the Planning Questions to guide students' thinking. Provide resource materials for students to share or have them gather their own.

7. Once groups have identified their concepts, ask them to think of their role, the challenges that may arise, and how their design will target the needs of both the animal and education as specified in their plan. Distribute the *Presentation Guide* (page 72) activity sheet, and ask students to think about and record the sequence in which they want to describe their design ideas to the class. Provide time for groups to rehearse their presentations. While they practice, circulate among the groups and provide feedback.

8. Tell students that as each group presents, students not involved in the presentation will act as the panel of administrators making the selection of what will be included in the new zoo exhibits. Invite groups to present their ideas to the panel. Direct each group to introduce the designers in their group and present their ideas in a dramatic presentation. During the presentation, the administrative panel should write down questions to ask during a question-and-answer period following the presentation.

9. Facilitate a final discussion in which designers and administrators note the features of the presentations that were most effective and compelling, focusing on the animal enrichment and public interest areas addressed.

10. Use the Questions for Discussion to debrief the experience.

Mantle of the Expert *(cont.)*

Planning Questions

- What do you know about this engineering problem?

- What do you need to know?

- What examples can you use from the real world?

- How can you explain the ways in which your exhibit will engage young people?

- How can you use your expertise as a zoo exhibit designer to convince administrators that this design deserves to be created?

- How will you present your ideas to show how the exhibit can engage the public?

- How will you use creative problem solving to solve the problem?

Questions for Discussion

- How did taking on the role of the expert feel? Why?

- How did it feel to be a member of the panel?

- In what ways was taking on the role of the designer different from presenting information as a student?

- Did you use ideas from other areas of science to help you solve the problem?

Specific Grade Level Ideas

K-2

Ask student exhibit designers to create a plan for an exhibit that highlights animal behavior on the playground. Have them sketch a map of the school playground with details, including, for example, the different habitats (bird nests, squirrel trees, picnic benches), and the other components that are embedded within the habitats on the playground (insects, tree diversity, shade area, sun, etc.). As a challenge, students can create and present imaginary playgrounds or add specific features to enhance existing structures.

Additional topics include designing a museum exhibit on racecars, or a park design targeting how to best capture daily temperature and sun/shade areas. See http://pbskids.org/designsquad/ for more ideas.

Mantle of the Expert *(cont.)*

3–5

Ask student exhibit designers to create an exhibit featuring a play habitat for the class (i.e., humans). They can create enrichment opportunities, figure out how the room will be organized, how many people are attending as visitors, and how many will be playing within each habitat. Students can judge the effectiveness of each element and how much time each might engage the students.

Additional topics could include more advanced engineering design challenges, such as a bridge design, a museum exhibit on simple machines, or a schoolyard weather station design.

6–8

Have students design habitat enrichment components for local animals, such as a butterfly garden, birdhouses, or bat boxes. Students can research what kind of food or nesting components are needed for that particular species within the local habitat and then determine the best area to add the enrichment components and observe the changes in behavior. Students can visit a zoo and analyze the particular exhibits of similar animals. They can do this ahead of time to consider the zoo exhibits as models, or after the fact to analyze the suitability of the exhibit as well as where the zoo environments are less than ideal.

Challenge students to design furniture from recycled cardboard, along with a garden area design focusing on local species selections.

9–12

Have students set up a bird observation station within your area, study the different types of feeders used, and watch and record the diversity of behaviors at the feeder. Send the data on bird types to the Cornell Lab of Ornithology to add to the long-term data collection efforts of citizen scientists around the world. As a way of further articulating their new understandings, have students create a visual map of the interrelationships and interdependencies among birds in their area.

Students could also design a water purification device or a museum exhibit on simple devices that target specific disabilities.

Zoo Director Memo

To: Zoo Exhibit Design Team
From: Zoo Director
Re: Animal Enrichment Design Idea Development

As you know, we have opened a new wing in the zoo for a new exhibit called *Engineered Conservation Habitats*. We want to develop several ideas about the exhibit, including how the exhibit will capture the excitement of conservation in an engaging way for students in your grade.

Your team has a history of creating exemplary exhibit designs. We are inviting you to present your ideas to our administrative team. Your exhibit should focus on the conservation of a single animal species and how it relates to other animals (butterflies, birds, bats, insects, etc.). Please find time to meet with your team, research habitat dynamics, and develop good examples of what might be included in your exhibit.

You will present your findings to an administrative panel in three weeks. Please be prepared not only to make a compelling case for your proposed exhibit and how it will engage young learners, but also to answer questions from the administrative panel. Good luck, and I look forward to hearing your creative conservation ideas.

Name _____   Date _____

Brainstorming Guide

Directions: Fill in the chart to organize your ideas for your exhibit. Attach sketches of potential layouts for your exhibit.

Animal Species:	
Habitat:	
Initial Ideas for Exhibit:	
Questions to Consider	**Ideas**
How will this idea be made engaging for the age group attending?	
How will you explain and represent the scientific ideas?	
How will visitors interact with the exhibit?	

Name _____ Date _____

Presentation Guide

Directions: Fill in the chart to organize your ideas for your exhibit presentation.

Presentation Title:		
Animal Species:		
Animal Habitat Design		
Drawings	Props	
Engineering Problem	Solution	
		_____ minutes
Visitor Education Focus		
Drawings	Props	
Scientific Concept	Exhibit Component	
		_____ minutes
		Total Time: _____ minutes

Teacher-in-Role

Model Lesson: The Designing Engineer

Model Lesson Overview

In this strategy, students imagine they are engineers who are skilled in designing new modes of transportation. Taking on the role of an engineer engages students in a meaningful exchange of ideas and sorting of scientific and technological information common to engineering work. This exchange allows the teacher and students to address common misconceptions.

Standards

K–2

- Knows that new tools and ways of doing things affect all aspects of life, and may have positive or negative effects on other people
- Plans and prepares improvisations
- Knows various ways of staging classroom dramatizations

3–5

- Knows that new inventions often lead to other new inventions and ways to do things
- Knows that new inventions reflect people's needs and wants, and when these change, technology changes to reflect the new needs and wants
- Knows how alternative ideas can be used to enhance character roles, environments, and situations

6–8

- Knows that scientific inquiry and technological design have similarities and differences
- Knows that science cannot answer all questions and technology cannot solve all human problems or meet all human needs
- Uses basic acting skills to develop characterizations that suggest artistic choices

9–12

- Knows that technology can benefit the environment by providing scientific information, providing new solutions to older problems, and reducing the negative consequences of existing technology
- Knows that mathematics, creativity, logic, and originality are all needed to improve technology
- Develops, communicates, and sustains characters that communicate with audiences in improvisations and informal or formal productions

Teacher-in-Role *(cont.)*

Materials

- *Design Engineer Script* (page 77, engineerscript.pdf)

- Engineer props (props for role and project bag with design examples)

- *Engineering Evidence Chart* (page 78, evidencechart.pdf)

Preparation

Review the *Design Engineer Script* (page 77) activity sheet so that you are comfortable in the role. Adapt the script as needed for your students and area of focus. Feel free to use a different speech pattern if you prefer—just make sure your delivery is different from usual to create a dramatic sense of character. As you invent your engineer persona, consider the following questions: *Who are you? What do you like? What might you wear?* Remember, you are a creative individual. You can make the activity more engaging by using props and dressing how the engineer that you invented might dress. Store props outside the classroom before you launch the activity. Your willingness to be dramatic will intrigue students and help them feel comfortable taking dramatic risks.

Gather images or small replicas of current modes of transportation, such as high-speed electric trains, automobiles (gas, hybrid, and electric), airplanes (with engines and glider), and rockets. Place them in a folder or box to share with students. Additional suggestions are provided in the Specific Grade Level Ideas.

Procedure

1. Tell students that they will enter a drama that invites them to design and engineer a new method of transportation called *New Motion* that relies on renewable energy sources. Tell students that the scene will begin when you say "Curtain up" and end when you say "Curtain down."

2. Excuse yourself from the room and put on your engineer outfit. Say "Curtain up" as you enter, letting students know that the drama is beginning. Clearly transition into the engineer role as you introduce yourself. Present the challenge to students using the *Design Engineer Script* (page 77) activity sheet.

3. End the drama by telling students that their teacher is returning, but you'll be back tomorrow at the same time to see what they have collected. Say "Curtain down" and leave the room when you are done to alert students the drama is ending. You can return later in role as the engineer to discuss the scientific and engineering concepts students arrived at in their designs.

4. Provide students time to collect images and information about current modes of transportation and to design the new method of transportation, *New Motion*. You may extend the activity throughout the day by allowing students to find examples in other parts of the school and at home.

Teacher-in-Role *(cont.)*

5. Return to class in the engineer role, and invite students to present their design ideas. Encourage students to report in the role of experts and use their designs to convince you and their peers of their ideas. During the presentations, display the *Engineering Evidence Chart* (page 78) activity sheet and use it to catalogue the designs as students present their findings. Invite other student engineers to weigh in on the discussion of designs, developing the collective knowledge of the group. Continue to add words, phrases, and significant ideas to the *Engineering Evidence Chart* activity sheet.

6. Challenge students' thinking by returning to class in the role of engineer and asking follow-up questions, such as, "Can you help me identify the fastest mode of transportation that you found?" "Can you explain how you were effective in creating so many new designs?" "It has been said that some motion takes no energy to produce. What can we say to stop this rumor?"

7. Use the Questions for Discussion to explore how the various roles supported students' learning.

Questions for Discussion

- How did you act differently when you were in the engineer role?

- On what did you base your ideas about what an engineer might be like?

- How did being in the engineer role help you think in new ways about the information and the work?

- How was the teacher in the engineer role different from the teacher in the teacher role?

Specific Grade Level Ideas

K–2

Students can design fantasy vehicles, such as rocket ships, and imagine the effect these new vehicles would have on their own lives. How would the roads have to change? Could they travel to see loved ones far away in one second? How would this impact their lives? It may also be helpful to review the meaning of the word *expert* prior to this activity and to give students the opportunity to identify some ways in which they are experts. As one student suggested, "In my family, I am the expert at making my baby sister laugh." At this level, the design engineer might be a puppet that visits regularly during the course of the year, looking for examples of scientific concepts being studied at that time. This strategy can also be used to investigate the expertise of other scientists such as a botanist looking at the variations of plants in their local area.

Teacher-in-Role *(cont.)*

3–5

Discuss the role of experts and engineers prior to the activity. Ask students what they know about experts and engineers and how they can be identified. Be sure to discuss the needs and desires new technology will address. As they develop their designs, students may want to look at how our needs have changed as they look at existing technologies and where they fall short. Ask students to consider how these technologies could be used in other unexpected ways.

This strategy can also be used to imagine other challenges such as a geologist investigating new ways to extract renewable energy from the earth.

6–8

Students can collect engineering design ideas from newspapers and store flyers. Challenge students to mirror the scientific inquiry method as they work on their designs. Have them propose solutions, develop some sketches, and investigate the scientific concepts behind their design. Does the scientific data support the feasibility of their design? Are there unintended consequences with significant negative impact? Once they have developed their designs, they can present their own design engineering role-play to younger students.

The strategy could be used to teach other content areas such as cell biology where the teacher takes on the role of a cell biologist searching for gene-based medical remedies.

9–12

Have students investigate different modes of transportation by analyzing the progression of technological improvements in terms of speed, efficiency, and sustainability. In doing this, students can track mankind's use of renewable and nonrenewable resources as it relates to modes of transportation (e.g., a shipbuilder's use of wood, a sailor's use of wind power, the use of fossil fuels to power automobiles, or a steam locomotive's use of coal). Then, students can offer proposed improvements to these modes of transportation in the role of experts from the time period. If desired, group students according to the criteria they will investigate (e.g., speed, efficiency, sustainability, or mode of transportation), and have groups compare and contrast their findings about transportation technology over time and sustainable transportation practices.

Design Engineer Script

Curtain up.

(Engineer peers around the corner curiously, as if looking for something.)

Good! You have arrived. Mr(s). *(insert teacher's name)* told me you would be here and be ready to work on my design. I need your help!

I am a design engineer. Who knows what a design engineer does? I have been asked to design *(looks confused as if trying to recall important information)* a new method of transportation, *New Motion*! That's right. *New Motion*, a new form of locomotion, a new mode of transportation. I am not entirely sure if I know exactly what that might be, but never fear! Design engineers design!

I really hope that you will join me as design engineers in training. You will learn that it takes great observation and focus to be a designer. You never know what you will be asked to find. People, things, scientific and technological information of all kinds….

(Looks around the room carefully) Perhaps you know what locomotion is. And you might also know some current forms of transportation. Well, I really need your help. You see, I have one tiny problem. I…well…that's the thing I never quite learned in school, so I really don't know what to look for! Will you help me?

I need to know what locomotion looks like and what forms of transportation are in use now. How will I recognize them? I need this information so I can—so we can design *New Motion*. Can you help? Just to make sure we are on the same page, let's list the characteristics of locomotion and transportation that we need to know for *New Motion*.

(Discussion ensues as the engineer works with students to determine where they may find examples of locomotion that transport people. As student engineers make relevant points, sharing their knowledge about concepts and examples, the design engineer takes notes on the board. These words and phrases can be referred to when they return together with examples of locomotion in hand.)

Great! Thank you! I now know what I am looking for. I think I have a few examples in my bag that fit the description of the evidence you have described. Let's see….

(At this point, the engineer can pull out examples and share them to solidify students' understanding of what they are looking for.)

Your job is to locate and document examples of transportation and locomotion, and then you must design new modes of transportation or *New Motion*. You will work in groups. We will meet later to share what we have found.

But shhhh! Your teacher is coming back—can we keep my mission a secret? Will you help me find examples of locomotion so we can design *New Motion*? See you tomorrow. Oh, and good luck!

Curtain down.

Name _____   Date _____

Engineering Evidence Chart

Directions: Complete the chart.

Engineering Content:	
Description of Design Evidence	**Description of Engineering Concepts**

Tableaux

Model Lesson: Sculpting the Changing Environment

Model Lesson Overview

In this strategy, students create *tableaux*, a French word meaning "frozen pictures," to create a tangible representation of factors that affect the health of a particular environment. By building a sculpture with their bodies, students investigate and represent ways in which humans impact the environment.

Standards

K–2
- Knows environmental and external factors that affect individual and community health
- Knows sources and causes of pollution in the community
- Selects interrelated characters, environments, and situations for simple dramatizations

3–5
- Knows the ways in which the physical environment is stressed by human activities
- Knows the ways people alter the physical environment
- Knows how visual elements and aural aspects are used to communicate locale and mood

6–8
- Understands the environmental consequences of people changing the physical environment
- Understands the origins and environmental impacts of renewable and nonrenewable resources, including energy sources like fossil fuels
- Creates characters, environments, and actions that create tension and suspense

9–12
- Knows the effects of biological magnification in ecosystems (e.g., the increase in contaminants in succeeding levels of the food chain and the consequences for different life forms)
- Constructs imaginative scripts that convey story and meaning to an audience

Materials

- Images that show human impact on the environment
- *Gallery Walk Observation Sheet* (page 84, gallerywalk.pdf)

Tableaux *(cont.)*

Preparation

Decide the specific content on which students will focus. Find images that students can draw from for information about the impact of humans on the environment, including purposeful changes to landscape, such as irrigation, or unintended consequences, such as deforestation or pollution.

Think about how to group students so that more complex ideas can be represented. Students can be asked to create individual tableaux, work in small groups, or represent more complex ideas best portrayed in larger groups of 5 or 6 students. In group tableaux, ask one student to act as "sculptor" by guiding the creation of a tableau. Select concepts and identify group size before beginning.

As this activity involves physical interaction, you may also wish to review respectful ways to work together. For example, you might note, "Show your 'clay' how you want them to position themselves through demonstration or by describing in words." Additional suggestions are provided in the Specific Grade Level Ideas.

Procedure

1. Introduce students to the particular environmental content on which they will focus. Share images that depict some of these processes, and ask students to discuss what may have happened before each image was taken. How might the scene have looked different? What do you think happened? How has it changed?

2. Introduce what a *tableau* is by inviting two students to join you in front of the class. Dramatize being a sculptor as you "mold" students into an environmental concept. You can facilitate this by describing how you want them to position their bodies or by modeling for them so that they can mirror what you do. For example, invite one student to stand tall with his or her arms spread open as if he or she were the branches of a living tree. Invite the other student to bend at the waist with wilted arms to represent a felled tree. Ask the viewers to identify the illustrated concept.

3. To further demonstrate the concept of a tableau, invite five students to the front of the room and suggest that they arrange themselves to form a variety of activities that change our physical environment and the climate. For example, one student could be planting crops in the soil, another could be a builder, another could be driving a car, and another could be dumping garbage in the ocean. Have students talk about the differences between an individual tableau and a group tableau, and the differences between taking on the sculptor role and using group decision making.

Tableaux *(cont.)*

4. Divide students into groups and assign each group a specific environmental issue to illustrate through tableaux. Provide groups with resource materials or have them research images and text to inform their tableaux. Choose from the following grouping options:

- Have students work in pairs. One student is the "sculptor" and the other is "clay." The sculptor molds "clay" into a human sculpture representing an environmentally-related concept.

- Have students work in small groups. One or two group members go to the center of the room and begin the sculpture with a pose that represents a landscape or environment. The rest of the participants add on, one by one, to create a group sculpture depicting ongoing changes in the environment, until all group members are involved. Suggested terms to explore include *air pollution*, *deforestation*, and *ozone depletion*.

- For more complex ideas, have students create a "slide show" in which they create multiple tableaux that show a progression. Images are presented one right after the other. The presenters can say "Curtain down" and "Curtain up" between images, indicating that the viewers should close their eyes in between slides so that they see only the still images and not the movement between images. Viewers can share their thinking about what they have seen following each slideshow.

5. Once students have developed their ideas, have groups present their tableaux to the class. You might introduce this by saying, "Imagine we are in an art gallery. We will walk around and look at the sculptures. At each stop on our gallery walk, we will talk about what we see, brainstorm words we think of, and discuss how the tableau represents the concept."

6. Depending on the way the tableaux have developed, sculptors could demonstrate their molding of the clay or students could just get into formation. Distribute the *Gallery Walk Observation Sheet* (page 84) activity sheet and tell students, "We will use this to track the list of the words you use to describe what you see, and we will find out from our sculptors what the term is and how our guesses relate to the concept represented in the tableaux." Use the Questions for Discussion to guide students' thinking.

7. As you move around the gallery, have students continue listing words used to describe the tableaux. You may want to keep a record as well. You will end up with a rich list of adjectives, synonyms, and metaphors that will allow students to see the scientific concepts in new ways. Add to the list as each group describes their process of creating the tableaux. This is often where ideas are translated and realizations occur. Capturing students' language will reveal the connections they have made.

Tableaux *(cont.)*

Questions for Discussion

- What concept do you think is being represented and what emotion is conveyed?

- What words come to mind as you view the sculpture?

- What do you see in the sculpture that suggests change in the environment?

- What cause and effect relationships do you see embodied in the sculpture?

- What similarities and differences were there in the different sculptures of the same ideas?

- As you were creating your tableau, how did you choose to portray environmental impact and why?

- What shapes and lines did you use in your sculpture to create a mood?

- Which ideas were easy to illustrate? Which concepts were more challenging?

- How did the descriptions offered by the viewers of the tableaux match your ideas of the concept being presented and the emotions you wanted to evoke?

- In what ways did the responses expand on what was being represented?

Specific Grade Level Ideas

K–2

Ask students to consider where they see human traces in their own communities (houses, garbage, cut grass, etc.). Have students imagine what the area was like before houses were there. Provide them with vocabulary or concepts that are concrete and easy to enact (a carefully designed garden, a fence, etc.). Have them use their bodies to create shapes that represent physical objects that contribute to different forms of pollution (air, water, ground, sound, etc.). Provide students with the opportunity to embody the idea and then to develop the skills to hold a shape still.

This strategy can also be used to observe and demonstrate how plants grow and germinate as well as the factors that affect plant growth and development.

Tableaux *(cont.)*

3–5

Help students create a list of human activities that stress the physical environment, such as driving cars, disposing of waste in rivers, and generating electricity. You can also challenge students with a term such as *pollution*, which will require them to portray a general category and to recognize the underlying connection among several examples. Engage students in doing research to investigate the differences between purposeful interventions and unintended consequences. Have students consider the unintended consequences of purposeful interventions, such as dams or canals. Make the work interdisciplinary by inviting students to consider the social and historical consequences of such projects. This strategy can be used to depict anything that changes over time such as transformation of larvae or the slow process of rock formation and deterioration.

6–8

Engage students in larger and more abstract ideas such as ozone depletion or climate change. Provide a list of concepts they can research independently. Ask students to consider the impact of both renewable and nonrenewable resources and challenge them to come up with ideas that may have a positive environmental impact or that may reverse some of the damage. Ask them to create a sense of suspense as they investigate potential environmental crises, tension as they work through difficult solutions, and hopefulness as they find ways to avert future crises. This strategy can be used to investigate and represent larger environmental changes such as geological changes in the earth and the forces that cause them.

9–12

Have students focus on a particular ecosystem and the variable factors that negatively impact that ecosystem. For example, students can explore the causes and environmental impact of harmful algal blooms (HABs), which result from the increased presence of phytoplankton and cyanobacteria in coastal waters. Students can investigate the impact on human life, on the ecosystem itself (e.g., disruptions in food webs or mass mortality), on surrounding wildlife, and on socioeconomic motives (e.g., tourism, commercial fisheries, or public health). Or students could investigate the harmful effects of deforestation on major rain forests across the globe among other intricate ecosystems.

Name _____   Date _____

Gallery Walk Observation Sheet

Directions: As you observe the tableaux, record your observations in the chart below.

Observation Notes	Tableau 1	Tableau 2	Tableau 3
Words to describe the tableau			
Notes from the sculptor and "clay" about the process			
Concept that is being represented			
What we've learned about the concept			

Monologue

Model Lesson: Meet Jane Goodall

Model Lesson Overview

In this lesson, students use monologue to deeply understand a famous person or character within the field of science or engineering to learn about the diversity of the many people, places, and teams that play important roles in the discovery process. Using information from a variety of sources, students write and perform a monologue in which they take the perspective of a famous figure. Speaking directly to the audience, students reveal a conflict, a choice to be made, or a problem to be resolved.

Standards

K–2

- Knows that in science it is helpful to work with a team and share findings with others

- Knows that students can do science

- Creates and acts out the roles of characters from familiar stories

3–5

- Knows that people of all ages, backgrounds, and groups have made contributions to science and technology throughout history

- Assumes roles that exhibit concentration and contribute to the action of dramatizations based on personal experience and heritage, imagination, literature, and history

6–8

- Knows that people of all backgrounds and with diverse interests, talents, qualities, and motivations engage in fields of science and engineering; some of these people work in teams and others work alone, but all communicate extensively with others

- Knows various settings in which scientists and engineers may work

- Uses basic acting skills to develop characterizations that suggest artistic choices

9–12

- Understands that science involves different types of work in many different disciplines

- Understands that individuals and teams contribute to science and engineering at different levels of complexity

- Develops, communicates, and sustains characters that communicate with audiences in improvisations and informal or formal productions

Monologue *(cont.)*

Materials

- A collection of texts about your chosen scientific figure

- *Affecting History* (page 90, affectinghistory.pdf)

- *Sample Monologue 1: Jane Goodall* (page 91, monologue1.pdf) or *Sample Monologue 2: Jane Goodall* (page 92, monologue2.pdf)

- *Monologue Planner* (page 93, monologueplanner.pdf)

Preparation

Gather a collection of texts by different authors that focus on scientific figures. The collection may include biographies, research articles, historical fiction, poetry, primary sources, etc. Subjects could include current scientific researchers, such as Jane Goodall, Katy Payne, E. O. Wilson, Stephen Hawking, or Tyrone Hayes, or historical figures, such as Diane Fossey, Rosalind Franklin, or Rachel Carson.

Using *Sample Monologue 1: Jane Goodall* (page 91) or *Sample Monologue 2: Jane Goodall* (page 92), whichever is developmentally appropriate for your students, practice reading the monologue aloud or select an example from literature to share with students. If students are not familiar with what a monologue is, share a selection from a familiar play or movie. You might find resources such as *Magnificent Monologues for Kids 2* by Chambers Stevens and *Minute Monologues for Kids* by Ruth Mae Roddy to be helpful. Additional suggestions are provided in the Specific Grade Level Ideas.

Procedure

1. Divide students into groups and assign groups a scientific figure to explore through monologue. Distribute the *Affecting History* (page 90) activity sheet to each group. Explain to students that they will research a historical figure by using multiple sources and considering different perspectives. Provide students with access to the collection of resources about the subjects and direct students to review several sources of information about the same person and record their findings on the *Affecting History* activity sheet. Circulate and facilitate group work as needed.

2. Bring the class together to share students' work. Tell students that they will present the information they learned through monologue. Talk with students about how a monologue is different from a dialogue.

Monologue *(cont.)*

3. Read *Sample Monologue 1: Jane Goodall* (page 91), *Sample Monologue 2: Jane Goodall* (page 92), or read your chosen example monologue to students *without* dramatic flair. Then, reread the monologue, asking students to close their eyes and visualize the character as you add dramatic flair to the reading. How might the character look, talk, move, or behave? Ask students for suggestions on how you could read the monologue dramatically. For example, when might you change your voice, make a gesture, move, pause, or otherwise dramatize the reading? Model these ideas in another reading of the monologue. Discuss what students were able to learn about the character through the monologue and the way it was presented.

4. Distribute the *Monologue Planner* (page 93) activity sheet and provide time for students to begin planning their individual monologues.

5. Have students share their monologue ideas with their group and think about which ideas suggest a conflict, which ideas could lead to effective dramatization, and which ideas might suggest humor or emotion.

6. Provide time for students to develop their monologues based on their expanded ideas.

7. Have students present their monologues to the class. Debrief the monologues, using the Questions for Discussion.

Questions for Discussion

- What insights did you gain into the character?

- What character traits came through?

- What is the character wrestling with?

- What emotions did you feel as you experienced the monologue?

- Where do you see the character traits (e.g., boldness) come through in the monologue?

- In what ways does the character stay true to his or her ideals?

- What sources were helpful? What biases did you discover?

- Now that you know the character, are there other motivations that come to mind that could inform his or her future choices?

- Did the character take risks to solve a problem? How?

Monologue *(cont.)*

Specific Grade Level Ideas

K–2

The activity can be more improvisational for younger students. When giving students a specific context, it helps them to consider how their character would react in that situation. Assign students a science subject that they have prior knowledge of, such as an author or an animal you have studied. Ask students to imagine they are entering a party where nobody knows them. How would they introduce themselves as the character? What is important about how they look or where they can be found? Students can begin their monologues by saying, "Hi, I'm (name of character). Let me tell you a bit about myself." Imagine that the character has something important on his or her mind. What might it be?

Students can create monologues about things other than people, such as plants, animals, rocks, or planets.

3–5

Students may choose to perform their monologues and put on a show for invited guests. Help them practice improvising their monologue. Allow them to write their monologues on index cards so that memorizing the lines doesn't become more important than the exploration of character. Once students become deeply familiar with a character through rehearsing their monologue, they will be able to accurately improvise the piece. Having index cards available may help the performers relax as they share their work with an audience. Have students create monologues from the perspective of inanimate objects involved in Jane Goodall's studies, such as the camera or the pencil recording the behavior of the chimpanzees or the tree where the chimps rest at night.

Monologue *(cont.)*

6–8

Have students create monologues from the point of view of other people, things, or settings in their character's life, such as Tyrone Hayes's microscope, a chimpanzee within a troop studied by Jane Goodall, or Stephen Hawking's computer. Explore people from the same period in history or the same profession and invite students to write monologues from their points of view. Compare the character traits of these people through monologue.

9–12

Have students consider the work that goes into scientific and engineering research by identifying individuals often not mentioned in research teams, such as Rosalind Franklin in the discovery of the DNA double helix, the team of researchers supporting Jane Goodall, or the team supporting Stephen Hawking. Have the students explore monologue through the eyes of a team member.

Name _____   Date _____

Affecting History

Directions: Complete the chart to learn about a scientific figure and to consider the sources of information.

Historical figure: _____

Describe the source of information.	Describe the scientific figure's character traits, his or her ideas, what actions he or she took, and other important information.	How does this information compare to information from other sources? How does this compare to what you already know?

Sample Monologue 1: Jane Goodall

So, you want to hear my story? It's hard to sum it all up in the time we have, but I'm happy to reflect back on it. It's been a wonderful life. I was born in 1934. I became a famous primatologist at a time when men dominated the field of science. I paved the way for other female researchers and am most known for my work with chimpanzees and conservation education. I began to live in the jungles of Gombe, Tanzania, in 1960 to study the behavior of chimpanzees and have continued to study the chimpanzee families within that region for 45 years with the help of my research team. I always knew that I was an animal behavior researcher, even when others told me that women should not be in the field.

Sample Monologue 2: Jane Goodall

Biography: Jane Goodall was born in London, England, in April of 1934. A famous primatologist, she is considered the world's leading expert on chimpanzees. Jane began to study wild chimpanzees in Gombe, Tanzania, without a college degree during a time when men dominated the field. She quickly became one of the leading researchers through her detailed observations that shed light on social and family dynamics that other trained scientists might have overlooked.

(Jane Goodall holds a letter, turns it over, and reads the sender's address.)

The great photographer Baron Hugo van Lawick. Hmm, I wonder—April 4, 1960—just two months to arrive and sent just a day after my birthday. *(She smiles slightly.)*

(She opens the letter.) Well I'll be. One brief visit and he's reaching out. Good! My work has sparked his attention.

(She reads a quote from the letter.) "I can't stop thinking about your observations and work with the chimps. Ms. Goodall, you intrigue me. You see the world in a way that is unique—through a different primate language."

(laughs) Too true, and I've been having this type of experience all my life. How is it that he recognizes my connection so quickly, so fully?

(She reads on.) "You must allow me to visit and capture some of the magic on film. Won't you let me come? *(pausing)* Please consider it. I will raise the funding I need for the trip. Your work should be broadcast to the world."

Broadcast to the world. *(She looks out the window.)* Perhaps this *is* what's needed. I am well aware, sir, that I live in a time when society does not deem it proper for women to be respected scientists. I've heard again and again that the jungle is not the proper place for a woman. Women aren't meant to be primatologists. Ridiculous! I have never followed the mainstream. But you see me. You understand my work.

I remember my first chimpanzee-like toy, Jubilee, given to me by my father. I could feel the excitement coursing through my veins—my love for animals and sense of adventure in my own backyard. I have that feeling now and the sense that my life is unfolding. My fingers are trembling. Baron Hugo van Lawick, he intrigues me. His style is distinctive. He's a pioneer as I am. Though it's easier for a man to pursue his vision, he recognizes my view of the world.

Baron Hugo van Lawick, I accept your proposal. *(She sighs with anticipation and looks into the distance.)* Jane Goodall the Primatologist.

Tonight I'll sleep under the stars with the sounds of the jungle in the distance. It will be hard to share this with the world. The spirit of the land here inspires me. The forest, the wind, the sky…there's no other place I feel so at home. Nature is my true company. But this Baron Hugo van Lawick. Maybe he can make my research reach a broader audience.

(She gathers her things and strides confidently out of her tent.)

Name _____ Date _____

Monologue Planner

Directions: Answer the questions to help plan your monologue.

What character traits does the character show? How?	How old is your character? Where does he or she live?
What type of research does he or she do? In what setting (with a team, in a lab, out in the field)? How is this important?	What challenge, decision, or dilemma does the character face?
What is the character trying to reveal?	How does the character feel about what he or she is saying? What facial expressions and body stances would portray this feeling?
How will your voice change during the monologue to reflect emotion and character?	What will the character realize at the end of the monologue?

Improvisation

Model Lesson: House on the Moon

Model Lesson Overview

Students consider what it would be like to live in a house on the moon. As they prepare for improvisation, students use their imagination, character research, and their investigation of materials, images, and texts that inform their understanding of gravity to develop an improvisation about going through daily routines in reduced gravity.

Standards

K–2

- Knows that things near the Earth fall to the ground unless something holds them up

- Understands that a model of something is different from the real thing but can be used to learn something about the real thing

- Plans and prepares improvisations

3–5

- Knows that the Earth's gravity pulls any object toward it without touching it

- Understands that models can be used to represent and predict changes in objects, events, and processes

- Plans and records improvisations based on personal experience and heritage, imagination, literature, and history

6–8

- Understands general concepts related to gravitational force

- Knows that models are often used to think about things that cannot be observed or investigated directly

- Creates improvisations and scripted scenes based on personal experience and heritage, imagination, literature, and history

Materials

- Collection of reference materials about astronauts

- *Explore the Character* (pages 97–98, explorecharacter.pdf)

Improvisation *(cont.)*

Preparation

Gather images or videos of astronauts living and working in space with much less gravity than on Earth. An Internet search will yield many pictures, articles, and videos about the effects of gravity and what happens when there is much less gravity. Gather a collection of props for being an astronaut and living on the moon. Additional suggestions are provided in the Specific Grade Level Ideas.

Procedure

1. Begin by asking students to think about their morning. Have them share the different things they did before arriving at school. Ask, "Did you get out of bed? Did you eat breakfast? Where did you sit when eating breakfast? Did you brush your teeth?"

2. Ask students to imagine those same activities as if they were living in a house on the moon. Have the class share ideas. After a few thoughts have been shared, remind the class that there would be much less gravity. Ask students what they know about gravity and what may happen with very little gravity.

3. Share with students articles, images, or videos about astronauts living in reduced gravity or microgravity.

4. As a class, discuss the differences in daily activities between living on Earth and the moon (e.g., brushing teeth, taking a shower, sleeping, eating, or going to the bathroom). Record student responses so they can refer to them throughout the lesson.

5. Ask students to choose one of the activities listed. Explain to students that *improvisation* is acting without a script in a spontaneous way. Model the use of improvisation to show what the character might be thinking or saying while performing this activity in a house on the moon with reduced gravity. Create a scene with a clear beginning, middle, and end that depicts what life would be like (the comedies and the challenges) without gravity. Act out the scene and use words that come to mind based on what you know about the concept and the emotions that the person may feel while performing this activity because of reduced gravity.

6. Divide students into pairs and assign each pair one of the activities from the list. Have pairs work together to decide how astronauts would perform their assigned activity and solve any related problems. Distribute the *Explore the Character* (pages 97–98) activity sheet to support students as they plan for improvisation.

7. Invite partners to share their improvisations with the class. Discuss the scenes, using the Questions for Discussion.

Improvisation *(cont.)*

Questions for Discussion

- What choices were made that brought the activity to life?

- What concepts were demonstrated through the improvisation?

- How did improvisation help you better understand gravity?

- What did the improvisation tell you about the story and the situation that the materials did not?

- Did you use ideas from other areas of science to inform your understanding of science concepts?

Specific Grade Level Ideas

K–2

Introduce students to how engineers had to research some of the solutions to the issues related to reduced gravity. Show pictures or video of astronauts sleeping or eating food in reduced gravity. Have students use improvisation to act out characteristics of different species or roles of different types of scientists, engineers, or research teams.

3–5

As an extension, invite students to create scenes and document their improvisations in written form, noting the back-and-forth dialogue and description of action. Ask them to describe how gravity works and what the impact of gravity can be in various circumstances. They can imagine if they were in a large, dense planet, how gravity might affect their daily lives. Other topics can include the water cycle, life cycles of different insects, or the movement of energy or planets within the solar system.

6–8

Have students improvise scenes based on research they conduct. Invite students to choose an astronaut from the International Space Station to research, and challenge them to become the character while investigating some of the issues they had in their space journey. Allow students to research alternative solutions that may have not made the cut yet to be included in the space station. Other topics include Earth's history, systems of living things, or the engineering design process within different forms of technologies.

Name _____ Date _____

Explore the Character

Directions: Complete the chart to examine what motivates a character to act in a certain way.

What character or personality traits does the main character show? What evidence in the materials makes you think this?	How do the character's traits help him or her to solve the problem or overcome a challenge or prevent him or her from doing so?
What are the character's feelings? What evidence in the materials makes you think this?	How do the character's feelings affect the events of the story?

Explore the Character *(cont.)*

Consider how the character would feel or act with (a) different:

- setting

- circumstances

- problem

- adventure

- character or personality traits

What might the character say and do in these situations? What dilemmas might the character encounter due to lack of gravity?

What risks might your character take in creatively solving a problem?

 #51086—*Strategies to Integrate the Arts in Science* © *Shell Education*

Music

Music

Understanding Music

Music has played a significant role in every culture since the beginning of time. Due to recent technology, our favorite tunes are readily available to us, and music has become even more prevalent in our lives. Dr. Howard Gardner has identified musical intelligence as one form of intelligence (2011). His theory of multiple intelligences suggests that students learn in different ways, and for some students, connecting with rhythm, beat, and melody provides access to learning. And as any adult who has introduced a cleanup song knows, music can motivate children and help them make transitions from one activity to another. Recently, attention has been given to the benefits of music in academic performance. It has been suggested that early music training develops language skills, spatial relations, and memory (Perret and Fox 2006). Paquette and Rieg also note that incorporating music into the early childhood classroom is particularly beneficial to English language learners' literacy development (2008).

Music and the sciences have long been linked. From the sounds of birdsong to the physical characteristics of musical instruments that shape their particular tone and timbre, scientific concepts have helped us understand how sounds and music are created, shaped, and changed.

In the strategies for this section, students explore scientific ideas alongside the basic elements of music and sound. Students engage in singing, playing, and composing music as well as making an instrument. The focus is on deepening scientific knowledge while experiencing the joy of creating music together in ways in which all students participate. Along the way, students develop a deeper understanding of and skills in creating music. No previous musical training is needed for you or your students.

Exploring scientific ideas through music engages and motivates students. As students identify, apply, and generalize ideas to real world situations, scientific concepts become meaningful and purposeful. Abstract ideas are connected to concrete models and students' representational fluency deepens. The more avenues we provide for students to experience the sciences, the more likely we are to connect with the variable ways in which students learn.

Music (cont.)

Strategies for Music

ꙮ Found Sounds

Sounds are all around us; they are found when we attend to them or manipulate them. Think about the sound of light rain or the squeals of delight you hear near a playground. There is rhythm in these sounds. Composer R. Murray Schafer thinks about the world as a musical composition. He notes, "In [music] we try to get people to use their senses to listen carefully, to look carefully" (quoted in New 2009). What makes sounds music rather than noise may depend on the listener, but it is also related to pitch (high or low) and rhythm. When students collect found sounds, they gain a new appreciation for what music is and develop careful listening skills. They can also better understand the environment from which sounds come. Students can categorize these sounds, experiment with making them, and explore their dynamics (volume). Their findings can be represented in graphic ways.

ꙮ Sampling

When a musical composition is sampled, a small portion of that music is taken and repurposed into a different song or piece to gain a new meaning. Made popular by the rise of electronic instruments and sound recorders, sampling is a major element in hip-hop and rap. It primarily involves reusing elements, or "samples," of audio or instrumentation from popular music or sound bytes from the Internet and television. A sample can be constructed as a loop or a rhythmic portion of something, or it can be the repetition of larger phrases in a music composition. Henry Jenkins notes in his text on media education in the 21st century, "Many of the forms of expression that are most important to American youths accent this sampling and remixing process, in part because digitalization makes it much easier to combine and repurpose media content than ever before" (2009, 32).

ꙮ Scoring

When music is composed, it needs to be scored so that others can perform it. Scoring is the communication of the sounds that are to be made and the timing of those sounds. The scoring can be done in nontraditional ways so that all learners are able to participate; for example, students can record a word in writing, such as *clap*, or draw a hand or other symbol to indicate when such a sound is to be made. Such scoring techniques allow students to construct the symbols and their meaning. Traditional scoring can also be considered, allowing students to experiment with the common language of musicians. Musical elements such as rhythm, tempo, volume, melody, and harmony relate to the scientific concepts such as temporal change, wave theory, states and characteristics of matter, and viscosity.

Music (cont.)

Instrumentation

This strategy focuses on the instruments used within a composition. Students can investigate the ways in which sounds are made, explore the skills needed to play different instruments, compare the different sounds instruments can make, and analyze the impact of different instruments within a musical piece. They can also construct their own instruments and experiment with how choices in their construction impact the sound that is made. As noted by Jeanne Bamberger (2000), "the question 'I wonder why that happened?' becomes the basis for interrogation, reflection and experimenting, and thus eventually for new ideas" (33). Students apply their knowledge of the composition and characteristics of materials (strength, density, hardness, and flexibility) as they make their instruments.

Chants

Chants involve the rhythmic repetition of sounds or words. They can be sung or spoken. They can be a component of spiritual practices or heard on a football field. By combining different dynamics (ranging from soft to loud), pitch (variations from high to low), and different notes (length of duration), students can create engaging sound effects that help them learn and remember ideas. According to Sonja Dunn (1999), "a chant is a rhythmic group recitation." Chants can be used in a variety of ways. They can be created with catchy rhythms that make the associated words easy to learn and remember. When this form of chants is emphasized, students retain important scientific information. Chants also can be constructed by layering phrases on top of each other that are then spoken or sung simultaneously. In this format, the use of differing rhythms and pitch create interest and suggest relationships among the chosen phrases and thus the content being considered.

Found Sounds

Model Lesson: Noise on My Street

Model Lesson Overview

In this lesson, students listen to, gather, and categorize sounds in the school environment. They learn about dynamics, duration, and pitch, and they interpret how the sound is made. They perform music by re-creating the sounds through the creative use of materials and vocals and playing with the composition.

Standards

K–2

- Knows that learning can come from careful observations and experiments

- Knows that tools can be used to gather information and extend the senses

- Knows the source of a variety of sounds

3–5

- Knows that scientists' explanations about what happens in the world come partly from what they observe (evidence), and partly from how they interpret (inference) their observations

- Knows that pitch is the highness or lowness of a sound

- Performs on pitch, in rhythm, with appropriate dynamics and timbre, and maintains a steady tempo

6–8

- Knows that sounds move at different speeds in different materials

- Uses appropriate tools and techniques to gather, analyze, and interpret scientific data

- Knows how the elements of music are used to achieve unity and variety, tension and release, and balance in musical composition

9–12

- Designs and conducts scientific investigations

- Uses technology and mathematics to perform accurate scientific investigations and communications

- Understands the ranges and traditional uses of various sound sources

Materials

- *Sound Observation Chart* (page 108, soundobservation.pdf)

- *Sound Categories* (page 109, soundcategories.pdf)

Found Sounds *(cont.)*

Preparation

Select a school location where students will be able to find many sounds, such as the playground, sports field, cafeteria, or another classroom. Practice the lesson on your own so you get a sense of what it feels like and what questions might arise. Additional suggestions are provided in the Specific Grade Level Ideas.

Procedure

1. Divide students into groups of 3 or 4 students and distribute the *Sound Observation Chart* (page 108) activity sheet to each group. Explain to students that they will be going to a location to listen to and observe sounds. Review the *Sound Observation Chart* activity sheet with students. Tell them they should find at least 8 sounds during their observation and describe and notate each sound on the *Sound Observation Chart* activity sheet.

2. Take students to the chosen location and give them approximately 15 minutes to work together to gather sounds and note them on the *Sound Observation Chart* activity sheet.

3. After returning to the classroom, have students share and compare their sound observations. Ask students to describe the qualities of the sounds they heard (e.g., the most common types of sounds, high or low sounds, quiet or loud sounds).

4. Introduce students to the following music vocabulary:

- *duration:* the length of time a sound is heard

- *dynamic:* variations of volume or loudness

- *form:* repetition, contrast, variation

- *pitch:* high or low sounds

- *texture:* layers of the sound

- *timbre:* characteristics of the sound itself

5. Ask students to name various sounds they found with respect to the *pitch* (high or low), the *duration* (short or long), and the *dynamic* (soft or loud) of the sound. Distribute the *Sound Categories* (page 109) activity sheet to each group and have students categorize their found sounds with respect to pitch, duration, and dynamics.

6. Have each student choose one sound from his or her group's observations. Tell students to practice re-creating their chosen sound using their bodies or voices.

Found Sounds *(cont.)*

7. Tell student groups to work together to create a composition using their individual sounds. Explain that sounds can be made one after the other or overlapped (texture). Students can experiment with musical form, playing with repetition, contrast, and variation. Students should pay attention to pitch, duration, and dynamic as they decide how to arrange the sounds.

8. Have each group perform their composition for the class. Use the Questions for Discussion to debrief.

Questions for Discussion

- What do you think caused the found sounds? How do you know?

- What did you notice about pitch, duration, and dynamic in the compositions?

- What artistic choices did you make when creating your compositions? What worked well? What might you change next time?

Specific Grade Level Ideas

K–2

Before collecting found sounds, spend time with students making loud sounds, soft sounds, high sounds, and low sounds. Students should collect just one or two sounds. Once sounds have been collected, have students identify from where their sounds came and have them pretend they are the source of the sound. This may help them more easily re-create the sound.

Students can also explore bird and animal sounds, talk about how animals and birds interrelate, and look at ecology rather than acoustics.

Found Sounds *(cont.)*

3–5

Students can find more sounds and perhaps each student can perform one sound that is high and one sound that is low. Their performance can be a little longer with a few more sounds. Extend this activity by having students use found objects to reproduce the sounds. Explain that sounds are vibrations and that pitch depends on the frequency of the vibrations. Give the analogy of throwing a pebble into a pond: the waves, or ripples, that result behave very much like sound waves—if the waves are close together, then the pitch of sound waves that are also close together would be high; if the waves are far apart, then the pitch of sound waves that are also far apart would be low. The taller the sound wave (i.e., "the closer together" concept from the pebble-wave analogy), the louder the sound. The shorter the sound wave (i.e., "the farther apart"), the quieter the sound.

Students can also explore how scientists use data collection in their work. They can use the strategy to expore how scientists collect samples, take measurements, and observe the natural world. Have them conduct a keyword search for "research stations in Antarctica" to provide them with a case study of scientific data collection at one of the research stations.

6–8

Students can gather sounds in the field with their cell phones or other recording software. When they return to the classroom, have them listen to their recordings and notate the sounds on the *Sound Observation Chart* activity sheet. Students can work together to create a longer and more nuanced composition, and they can give it a name.

Students can also explore how scientists use tools to extend their senses. For example, how do microscopes, binoculars, magnifying glasses, or telescopes allow scientists to observe things they ordinarily could not see?

9–12

Students can gather sounds in the field with their cell phones or other recording software. When they return to the classroom, have them listen to their recordings and notate the sounds on the *Sound Observation Chart* activity sheet. Students can also monitor sounds based on the time of the year, species, and habitat. Birds are said to change their pitch and duration of their call based on the surrounding noise (city street vs. park). Students can also use this strategy to identify specific species of birds and their respective sounds.

Name _____ Date _____

Sound Observation Chart

Directions: Use this chart to document the sounds you find during your sound exploration.

Group name: _____   Date: _____

Sound Name	Pitch (high or low)	Duration (how long)	Dynamic (loud or quiet)	Sound Source

Name _____   Date _____

Sound Categories

Directions: List the sounds you collected in the categories. Categorize each sound according to pitch, duration, and dynamic.

Pitch		
low	medium	high

Duration		
low	medium	high

Dynamic		
low	medium	high

Sampling

Model Lesson: The Human Weather Sampler

Model Lesson Overview

In this lesson, students read and listen to local weather reports by the National Weather Service (NWS) and the National Oceanic and Atmospheric Administration (NOAA). They "sample" portions of a given section by listening to and repeating phrases they hear. Students perform a short piece based on the weather patterns for that day, each taking turns playing the "human sampler."

Standards

K–2

- Knows that short-term weather conditions can change daily, and weather patterns change over the seasons

- Sings ostinatos, partner songs, and rounds

3–5

- Knows that water exists in the air in different forms and changes from one form to another through various processes

- Sings on pitch and in rhythm, with appropriate timbre, diction, and posture, and maintains a steady tempo

6–8

- Knows ways in which clouds affect weather and climate

- Sings music written in two and three parts

- Knows music that represents diverse genres and cultures

9–12

- Understands that individuals and teams contribute to science and engineering at different levels of complexity

- Arranges pieces for voices other than those for which the pieces were written in ways that preserve or enhance the expressive effect of the music

- Knows various roles that musicians perform and representative individuals who have functioned in these roles

Sampling *(cont.)*

Materials

- *Sampling and Sound* (page 115, samplingsound.pdf)
- Examples of sampled songs
- Index cards and pens or pencils
- "Sampling hat"

Preparation

Prior to the lesson, have students listen to a weather forecast for homework and write down key phrases about the weather they hear to bring to class.

Visit the National Weather Service website (http://forecast.weather.gov) and enter your zip code. Scroll down past the 7-Day Forecast and click on *Forecast Discussion*. Then, print the Forecast Discussion. (*Note:* Clicking the hyperlinked words in the Forecast Discussion will take you to the entry for each word in the National Weather Service glossary.)

Select examples of sampled songs to share with students. One well known example uses barking dogs to sing "Jingle Bells." An Internet search for "Jingle Bell Dogs" will yield many versions to sample.

Find or make a distinctive and easy-to-wear "sampling hat" or other engaging device to designate the student who is directing the group by "playing" the samples. Additional suggestions are provided in the Specific Grade Level Ideas.

Procedure

1. Ask students to share the weather-related phrases they heard in a weather report. Record these phrases for students to refer to throughout the lesson.

2. Read students the current National Weather Service Forecast Discussion for your region. When reading a Forecast Discussion from the National Weather Service website, the hyperlinked vocabulary will direct you to a glossary with a definition of the term. Be sure to emphasize this vocabulary.

3. Ask students if they hear any phrases from the Forecast Discussion that they heard the night before. Ask them if there is any difference between this report and the report they heard the night before. Add any new weather words or phrases to the recorded list.

Sampling *(cont.)*

4. Ask students to look at the underlined (or hyperlinked) words from the Forecast Discussion and think of a type of sound that weather might make that they could re-create with their bodies or voices. Distribute the *Sampling and Sound* (page 115) activity sheet to students and have them complete the chart. Have students demonstrate their ideas with partners.

5. Ask students if they know what *sampling* is. Explain that sampling is the taking of small portions of sound or music and mixing it with other sounds in a song. If desired, play examples of sampled songs for students.

6. Divide students into groups of 6 to 8. Ask students to work with their groups to select a short phrase from the weather report they heard, the Forecast Discussion, or a weather sound, being sure that each student has a weather "sample" to practice aloud. Students may use the *Sampling and Sound* activity sheet to guide them through this process.

7. Have students line up with their groups. Put on the "sampling hat." Tell students that whoever wears the "sampling hat" plays the different "weather samples." Select one of the groups, and tell the group that when you point to a student in the group, he or she will "play" his or her "sample" (i.e., they will make their selected weather sound). Each student represents only one sound. Meanwhile, have the rest of the students clap to a steady and slow beat. Once the beat is established, point to different students in the group to "play" their samples. Experiment with making a sampled song with each group.

8. When students are comfortable with the process, tell them that when you point lower, they should make their sound lower and slower. When you point higher, they should make their sound higher and faster. Practice with each group.

9. Let students take turns wearing the "sampling hat" and "playing" the samples to create unique compositions.

10. Use the Questions for Discussion to debrief the activity.

Sampling *(cont.)*

Questions for Discussion

- What did you learn about the weather from listening to the weather report?

- What weather words and phrases help describe weather patterns in specific ways?

- How did hearing the "weather samples" add to the weather vocabulary?

- What are your favorite weather phrases? Why? What do they mean?

Specific Grade Level Ideas

K–2

Instead of reading a Forecast Discussion, read aloud a weather report from the National Weather Service website and ask students what they think the report means. Give students key sounds and phrases to repeat, and rather than working in small groups, work as a whole class. Do this over a period of a week until students have internalized the basic weather vocabulary and concepts.

3–5

As an extension, have students find the definitions of the vocabulary words used by the National Weather Service and use those words in a weather report they invent.

This strategy can be used to explore vocabulary from any area of science.

6–8

Have students further develop their own music compositions, using electronic recording. If they have an iPhone® or iPad®, there are many sampling applications available, including Loopy. Students can easily sample weather words or phrases and play them back. There are also several free audio-recording apps available.

This strategy can also be used to explore vocabulary used in geology or earth science, and students can research the meaning of the vocabulary term. If the technology to record audio is not available, have students work in groups of 5 or 6 to create the "Human Looper" by repeating various words in groups.

Sampling *(cont.)*

9–12

Take advantage of the audio resources that NASA offers. There are many student and teacher resources on the NASA website. The Radio JOVE Project—an educational program designed for students to learn about radio astronomy—is very interesting, and audio from the Space Transportation System (STS) missions can be used by students to create their own sampling compositions based on NASA audio resources.

If students have a Mac or PC, Audacity is a free open source audio editor that students can use to layer their compositions.

Name _____ Date _____

Sampling and Sound

Directions: Complete the chart to help you think of ways to recreate the sounds weather can make.

Key vocabulary from the weather report or Forecast Discussion	Different sounds that weather can make	Ways I can recreate the sound with my body or voice

Scoring

Model Lesson: The Human Drum

Model Lesson Overview

In this lesson, students listen to and create a variety of percussive sounds with their hands, feet, and arms. They create symbolic notation for their original body percussion sounds, indicating the direction and speed of motion. Students use these symbolic notations to create a sound score for the human body.

Standards

K–2

- Knows that things move in many different ways

- Uses a variety of sound sources when composing

3–5

- Knows that an object's motion can be described by tracing and measuring its position over time

- Creates and arranges short songs and instrumental pieces within specified guidelines

6–8

- Knows that an object's motion can be described and represented graphically according to its position, direction of motion, and speed

- Understands effects of balanced and unbalanced forces on an object's motion

- Knows how the elements of music are used to achieve unity and variety, tension and release, and balance in musical compositions

Materials

- Video samples of human drumming and percussion

- *Human Percussion Notation* (page 120, humannotation.pdf)

- Large sheets of butcher paper

Preparation

Conduct an Internet search for videos of "body percussion" or "body drumming." View some videos to see a variety of styles, gestures, and uses of the body to make percussive music. Refer to the Recommended Resources in Appendix C for suggested videos. Select a few videos to share with students. Additional suggestions are provided in the Specific Grade Level Ideas.

Scoring *(cont.)*

Procedure

1. Model for students some different percussive sounds that can be made with the human body, such as snapping, clapping, stamping, and clapping with hollowed hands. Show students the videos of human drumming and percussion you located and discuss how body percussion is manifested around the world. What are differences? Similarities?

2. Review the concepts of *vibration* and *amplification* and ask students to think about how they relate to body percussion. For example, have students consider that the sound generated by flicking their cheek when their mouth is open is the *vibration* of the skin, *amplified* by the open mouth. The sound of a heartbeat is a vibration inside the body. Ask students, "What other parts of the body might provide good amplification?" As a class, brainstorm how students might notate the nuances of amplification in a score.

3. Gather students in a circle around the room. Go around the circle and ask each student to make a sound as a human percussive instrument. Have students identify the body part, direction of movement, and speed with which the movement is made for each sound. Have students experiment with changing the direction and speed of motion to see how it affects the sound produced.

4. Divide students into pairs. Ask each pair to create a percussive sound using their bodies. Ask each pair how many ways they can create percussive sounds using their hands or feet. Have them decide together on one sound. They should experiment with the direction and speed of their motion and the possibilities for amplification using the body until they are satisfied with the sound produced. Use the Planning Questions to stimulate students' thinking.

5. Distribute the *Human Percussion Notation* (page 120) activity sheet to students and have them create a symbol to tell others how to make their body percussion sound. Each symbol should indicate the body part that is making that sound, the direction of the motion, and the speed with which the motion is made. For example, a handclap could be notated by a drawing of two hands or more abstract representations with two arrows between the hands pointing towards each other, and a tight, zigzagging line to indicate the fast speed.

6. Display the groups' *Human Percussion Notation* activity sheets for all students to see. Have students share their notations with the class, demonstrate their sounds, and lead the class in making the percussive sounds they created.

7. Explain to students that they will create their own musical scores, using their percussive sounds. Tell them that a musical score is the written form of music. Divide students into groups of 4 and give each group a sheet of butcher paper. Have students develop a short composition by creating a musical score with their symbols by sequencing the sounds represented on the notation sheets.

Scoring *(cont.)*

8. Have students practice playing the notated sounds in various sequences until they arrive at a composition they are satisfied with. This will require some back-and-forth experimenting with the order of the sounds. Have them draw the notations on the butcher paper in the order they are to be played to create the musical score.

9. Tape the completed scores to the classroom wall and have the class perform each musical score.

10. Use the Questions for Discussion to debrief the activity.

Planning Questions

- How might you notate your composition to designate various qualities of sound, including amplification, tempo, and dynamics?

- How does changing the speed of motion affect the sound you are making?

- How does changing the angle of impact with a particular object or surface affect the sound you are making?

- How can you use the body to amplify your sound?

Questions for Discussion

- What did you learn about the sound you produced both musically and scientifically?

- How did the direction or speed of motion affect the sounds?

- How did you go about designing the symbol for your sound?

- What steps did you go through to develop the musical score?

- What did you find challenging about the final musical performance?

- Did putting the score together give you other ideas for musical pieces?

- Why might a musician or composer create a score?

Scoring *(cont.)*

Specific Grade Level Ideas

K–2

Have students focus on the production of human percussion sounds and identify how their body parts move as they experiment with the various sounds they can make. Students can create a simple symbol for their sound. For younger students, instead of developing a musical score on paper, lay the notation symbols in the middle of the circle and play various sequences. Students create the symbols individually and share how each symbol sounds. Then, pictures of the symbols are placed in the middle. The class experiments with making varying sequences of a few symbols at a time, and the class, as a group, "plays" the sequence together to see how it would sound as a musical piece. Students can refine the piece as they experiment. As an extension, you can add letters of the alphabet to the sequence and experiment with ways of pronouncing particular letter sounds as you integrate them into the sequence.

3–5

Provide some guidelines for students' compositions as they develop their score; for example, they must repeat at least one sound or they must create a repeating pattern of sounds. This strategy can also be used to help students learn anatomy or parts of the body.

6–8

Have students consider the effects of balanced or unbalanced forces on an object's motion with respect to the various sounds created by the body. Challenge students to compose a score that reflects unity and variety, tension and release, and balance. Have students create body percussion sounds and movements to show how the systems of the body work together as a whole.

Name _____ Date _____

Human Percussion Notation

Directions: Draw symbols in the chart that describe how to make your human percussion sound.

Percussive choices	Direction of motion	Speed of motion

In the space below, combine all three drawings to create a symbol or picture to show others how to make your human percussion sound.

Instrumentation

Model Lesson: The "Don't Throw it Away" Band

Model Lesson Overview

In this strategy, students learn about the properties of sound as they design and build musical instruments from recycled materials. They research the acoustic properties of the instrument to find out why it makes a specific kind of sound. Then, they give their instrument a name based on what they have learned about its sound properties.

Standards

K–2

- Knows that sound is produced by vibrating objects

- Plays with a variety of musical instruments

3–5

- Knows that the pitch of a sound depends on the frequency of the vibration producing it

- Knows advantages and disadvantages of recycling and reusing different types of materials

- Performs simple rhythmic patterns accurately and independently on rhythmic classroom instruments

6–8

- Knows that vibrations move at different speeds in different materials, have different wavelengths, and set up wave-like disturbances that spread away from the source

- Knows community programs for reusing or recycling materials

- Performs on instruments, alone and with others, a varied repertoire of music

9–12

- Understands that waves have characteristic properties and behaviors

- Knows issues related to the reuse of resources

- Uses ensemble skills when performing as part of a group

Materials

- Cleaned objects from home that would otherwise have been discarded

- video samples of recycled instruments

- *Instrument Design* (page 125, instrumentdesign.pdf)

- Craft materials, such as scissors, tape, glue, rubber bands, yarn, or wire

Instrumentation *(cont.)*

Preparation

Have students bring in 3 to 4 objects from home that would otherwise have been thrown away, such as small cardboard boxes, bottle caps, milk jugs, soda bottles, empty toilet paper or paper towel rolls, tin cans, etc. Tell students that the items must be clean and that cans must not have sharp edges. Conduct an Internet search for videos of "recycled instruments" and select videos of recycled instruments being played to share with students. Also conduct a key-word search for "instrument families" to familiarize yourself with the differences between wind, percussion, and stringed instruments. For younger students, it may be helpful to also explore "The Young Person's Guide to the Orchestra." Additional suggestions are provided in the Specific Grade Level Ideas.

Procedure

1. Gather all the objects students brought in from home in one place. Ask students if they know what happens to these objects in their community. Talk about the differences between reusing and recycling objects. Discuss the materials the objects are made from. Tell students that they are going to transform these objects into musical instruments.

2. Share videos of recycled instruments and ask students to listen carefully to the sounds. Ask them how they think the instruments make the sounds.

3. Ask students what they know about the differences between *wind instruments*, *percussion instruments*, and *stringed instruments*. Discuss vibration and describe how a sound wave works and how the sound reaches the ear.

4. Divide students into groups of 3 or 4, and invite them to imagine they are a band that will make its own instruments. Tell them that they will each design a wind instrument, a stringed instrument, or a percussion instrument, or they can make an instrument that can be played in more than one way. Distribute the *Instrument Design* (page 125) activity sheet and direct students to look over the available objects, using the worksheet to help them design an instrument.

5. Have each group present their instrument designs to the class. Ask them to describe the sounds they think their instrument will make and why. They can also talk about how they think the instruments will work together as a band.

6. Provide students with craft supplies to create their instruments using the discarded objects according to their designs.

7. Have students play their instruments and listen carefully to the sounds they make. Ask students to write a short description of the properties of the sound their instrument makes (i.e., dynamic, pitch, duration, etc.). How high is it? How low is it? Is it loud or soft? Is it a long, sustained sound or a short, staccato sound?

Instrumentation *(cont.)*

8. Talk with students about how to draw a sound wave that represents the properties of the sound their instrument makes. Share images of sound waves and compare characteristics of sound waves to characteristics of various sounds. Based on these observations, have students create visual inferences of what sound waves might look like for their instruments. Discuss how the sounds are different and why. Based on the sound properties of their instruments, ask students to give their instruments names.

9. Have each band work together to create a short composition using their instruments. Provide time for practice.

10. Have each band perform their composition for the class and present their instruments and sound wave drawings. Use the Questions for Discussion to debrief.

Questions for Discussion

- How is the sound of a percussion instrument different from a wind instrument or a stringed instrument?

- How different was the sound of your own instrument from what you expected?

- What were the different sound properties of the different kinds of instruments?

- How did the instruments' materials make a difference in the way they sounded?

- What did you discover about how the different sounds in the band worked together?

Specific Grade Level Ideas

K–2

Have students play with materials, such as rustling paper, to investigate the range of sounds they can make. You can give students specific instructions to build various kinds of instruments. Provide more supplementary materials, such as rubber bands and waxed paper, and make the instruments fairly simple to put together. Have students first play their completed instruments individually and then play together, focusing on rhythm as a means of performing. Students could also build instruments in pairs and take turns playing different kinds of instruments.

This strategy can also be used to develop instruments to investigate and replicate sounds in nature, such as water and wind, or other kinds of sounds related to animals.

Instrumentation *(cont.)*

3–5

Students can expand their knowledge about sound, vibration, the difference between high and low sounds, and how sounds change in relation to the materials used. Help students identify materials that can be used to accomplish a design through specific properties of shape, flexibility, etc. Have students describe what makes a material appropriate for the design task at hand. When students create music as a group, have them focus on rhythm and pitch as a means of performing.

6–8

Students can go deeper into the intricacies of acoustics and sound waves. They can also consider the context and space and how sound waves bounce or are absorbed. This strategy could also be used to investigate the relationships between sounds. For example, students can replicate and play the sounds of a particular context, such as a specific ecosystem, or students could investigate structures and properties of matter.

9–12

Have students use this strategy in a study on the physics of vibration. Students can identify the kind of sound wave their instrument produces by using an oscilloscope. If you don't have an oscilloscope, conduct an Internet search for "virtual oscilloscope" to find software that simulates an oscilloscope so students can see the sound wave. There are also apps, such as "Soundbeam," that simulate an oscilloscope.

Ask students what instruments they play and if they play in a band, and use this as an opportunity to discuss the materials used in creating their instruments. Compare their instruments with examples of instruments of different cultures in their material and design choices.

Name _____   Date _____

Instrument Design

Directions: Answer the questions.

1. What materials will you use to create your instrument?

   _____

   _____

2. How do you play this instrument?

   _____

   _____

3. Is it a stringed, percussion, or wind instrument, or a combination of these?

   _____

4. What kind of sound do you expect it to make?

   _____

   _____

5. What kind of sound wave will your instrument make?

   _____

Sketch the design of your instrument.	**Sketch how your instrument is played.**

Chants

Model Lesson: The Phyla of Life on Earth

Model Lesson Overview

Chanting is a musical strategy that can help students learn taxonomies in science. Using pitch and rhythm, students create musical compositions that help them learn various phrases and sentences common to scientific inquiry. In this lesson, students use chanting to learn about taxonomy and the scientific classification systems for living creatures.

Standards

K–2

- Knows that there are similarities and differences in the appearance and behavior of plants and animals

- Sings ostinatos, partner songs, and rounds

3–5

- Knows different ways in which living things can be grouped and purposes of different groupings

- Sings on pitch and in rhythm, with appropriate timbre, diction, and posture, and maintains a steady tempo

6–8

- Knows ways in which living things can be classified

- Sings with appropriate timbre, intonation, and diction at a level that includes modest ranges and changes of tempo, key, and meter

Materials

- Large roll of paper

- Painter's tape (that will stick and re-stick)

- *Tree of Life* (page 130, treelife.pdf)

- Poster board

- Thick, dark markers

Preparation

Prior to the lesson, have students find pictures of living creatures and bring them to class. These can be drawn, printed from the Internet, or cut out from a magazine. Additional suggestions are provided in the Specific Grade Level Ideas.

Chants (cont.)

Procedure

1. Lay a large sheet of paper on the floor and invite students to sit around it, bringing with them the images of living creatures they brought to class. Have students lay their images on the large paper. Talk about the different characteristics that living creatures share, and work together to sort and categorize the images into different groups. Encourage students to consider several kinds of grouping strategies.

2. Introduce students to the concept of taxonomy and classification, and decide as a class on one particular way of classifying the life forms according to the characteristics students identified. Have students sort the images into clearly defined groups on the large paper and tape the images in place with painter's tape.

3. Talk with students about the classification system of Kingdom-Phylum-Subphylum-Class-Order-Family-Genus-Species. Distribute the *Tree of Life* (page 130) activity sheet and review it with students. Talk about shared characteristics, and explain that the further down the Tree of Life they go, the fewer and fewer shared characteristics are found in each group.

4. Return to the initial grouping of the images students sorted. Ask students how their classification system is different from the Tree of Life and how it is similar. Assist students in grouping the images by kingdom or phylum.

5. Tell students that they will create chants about the Tree of Life classification system. Explain that in a chant, each line is sung or spoken by a group with a particular rhythmic pattern and pitch (high or low vocal tone). Introduce the musical term *ostinato* as a repetition of similar rhythmic patterns and tones.

6. As a class, do the simple chant, "Kingdom-Phylum-Subphylum-Class-Order-Family-Genus-Species." Introduce students to the term *pitch* (highness or lowness of a tone). Ask students to use a low voice for Kingdom, and as each word is chanted, have them use a slightly higher voice until they get to Species. At the end, have students clap three times. If desired, have students crouch low on the floor, slowing moving higher as their voices get higher as well. Then, have students repeat the chant in reverse from high voice to low voice until they return to Kingdom. Students should again clap three times. Next, introduce students to the concept of *rhythm* (repeating beat). Have students repeat the chant quickly and then slowly. Introduce students to the term *dynamics* (softness or loudness). Then, have students do the chant loudly and then softly. Finally, introduce students to the term *duration* (length of a sound or note) and have them repeat the chant by saying each word quickly, then by drawing the words out.

Chants (cont.)

7. Divide students into groups of 4 or 5. Assign each group a different kingdom classification: *Plantae*, *Animalia*, *Fungi*, *Protista*, and *Moneran*, which includes *Eubacteria* and *Archaebacteria*. Have students choose an organism in their assigned kingdom and research the names for the phylum, subphylum, class, order, family, genus, and species. Students will use these series of names for their chants.

8. Give each group a sheet of poster board and a thick, dark marker. Have each group prepare a chant based on the classification of their species and write it on the poster board. Ask students to practice using various elements of rhythm, pitch, and dynamics of sound. Circulate among the groups and use the Planning Questions to help students plan their chants.

9. Provide time for groups to rehearse their chants.

10. Bring the class together as a whole. Ask each group the name of their species, and then ask each group to display their poster and perform the chant. Use the Questions for Discussion to debrief the activity.

Planning Questions

- What pitch will you use?

- What dynamics will you use?

- What rhythms are suggested by the words in your line?

- What other sound effects might you add to give your phrase more interest (clapping, stomping, slapping the desk, and so forth)?

- Are there gestures you could add to emphasize your tempo (slow, curved motions or quick, jagged moves)?

Questions for Discussion

- What did you learn about the species you picked?

- How was it different from other species in its genus or family?

- Did anything surprise you in the sound of the names of the different classifications?

- Describe the musical aspects of your chant (beat, dynamics, pitch, duration).

- Why might a scientist want to classify living creatures?

- What are some other ideas you could use to make your chants more interesting?

Chants (cont.)

Specific Grade Level Ideas

K–2

Talk with students about what living creatures have in common and what things are different. As a group, create a chant based on students' ideas.

This strategy can be used to help students memorize other science concepts, such as the structure and function of organisms.

3–5

Give students a broad overview of the kingdoms as a classification system, and then ask them which kingdom they think the organism in their picture belongs to. Have students discuss which of the various animals or plants share characteristics and which are different. Divide students into pairs and have each pair choose one of the images of living creatures. Have each pair create a short chant about their creature and its characteristics and perform it for the class.

6–8

Students can delve deeper into the concept of biodiversity and how it is captured and categorized. This strategy can also be used to help students memorize other science concepts, such as characteristics of the Earth system—core, mantle, lithosphere, hydrosphere, and atmosphere.

Tree of Life

Animal (Animalia)

Plant (Plantae)

Kingdom

Phylum

Subphylum

Class

Order

Family

Genus

Species

Poetry

Poetry

Understanding Poetry

Poetry engages students in writing, reading, speaking, and listening. Creating poems can capture the essence of an idea. As stated by Polly Collins, "When students create poems about topics of study, they enhance their comprehension through the connections they have made between the topic and their own lives, the topic and the world around them, and the poetry and the content texts they have read" (2008, 83). Developing scientific understanding through the creation of poems allows students to consider science concepts in new ways and allows them to share their understanding through language and metaphor. Often, students enjoy creating poems but are not sure how to begin. The strategies in this section provide guidance that will help students identify and work with rich language to explore scientific ideas. Though poems often rhyme, they do not need to, and sentences do not need to always be complete. "We are more interested in 'surprising images' or words that have a special sound pattern. They empower students to be 'word-gatherers'" (McKim and Steinbergh 1992, 45). Students are invited to put words together in unconventional ways, drawing on evocative language, playful juxtaposition of ideas, and creating images through words as they write poems about concepts in science. This active engagement changes students' relationship with science as they find their own language to describe what they know and what they observe.

We tend to think about science as working with facts and formulas, and yet theoretical structures of science, its vocabulary, and the application to real-world situations are equally important for students to understand. By working with poetic language, symbolism and metaphor, students can deepen and articulate their understanding of scientific ideas. As Lipman Bers notes, "What makes a good poem—a great poem—is that there is a large amount of thought expressed in very few words" (quoted in Albers, Alexanderson, and Reid 1990).

Using poetry to explore scientific ideas builds conceptual understanding. When students become poets, they fine-tune their writing and explore the use of patterns, rhythm that is also found in scientific concepts, and metaphor, which has the capacity to make scientific principles visible. Writing poems allows students to use language in fresh ways to develop a deeper understanding of scientific ideas. As Arthur D. Efland (quoted in Stewart and Walker 2005) notes, "It is only in the arts where the processes and products of the imagination are encountered and explored in consciousness—where they become objects of inquiry, unlike in the sciences where the metaphors that are used remain hidden" (111).

Poetry *(cont.)*

Strategies for Poetry

❧ Dialogue Poems

Compare and contrast is one of the most effective instructional strategies that teachers can use (Marzano 2007). A dialogue poem encourages students to explore two different perspectives on a topic. This form of poetry works well with opposite but related concepts or perspectives. Similarities and differences between concepts can be explored, providing the rhythm and the feel of a dialogue. The poem is constructed by two writers, encouraging conversation about the content being explored and the ways to best translate ideas into poetic form. This collaborative work allows students to share what they know with their peers and to deepen learning. By juxtaposing two ideas or phenomena, it also has great potential to help students clarify their understanding by differentiating between related scientific concepts in ways that can address common misconceptions.

❧ Bio Poems

This biographical strategy allows students to investigate traditions, attitudes, environmental influences, and commonly held perceptions about science. Inspired by George Ella Lyon (2010), bio poems follow a pattern using the phrase *I am from* and can be created through student responses to prompts (Kuta 2003). Using the senses to reflect on what has been seen, heard, smelled, touched, and tasted, students become aware of how they (or characters, fictional or real) have been shaped by their unique experiences. The observations and reflections help students become aware of how time and place can influence one's perspectives. When written about themselves, students' bio poems can provide teachers with relevant background information about students' relationship to scientific knowledge, offer insights on how to best work with individual students to support their learning, and enhance student–teacher communication.

❧ Rhyme and Rhythm

This strategy invites students to work in verse as ideas are translated into rhyming words and phrases. Jan LaBonty notes that "a preference for rhyme and rhythm is contained in the linguistic make-up of all humans; rhyme is easier to recall than prose; rhythm helps carry the predictability of language. There is pattern and measure in every language and in the way we structure our lives" (1997). Though poems do not need to rhyme, rhymes can unify a poem and the repeated sound can help to connect a concept in one line to that in another. Also, simple rhymes can serve as a memory device (Jensen 2008) for scientific concepts, and students are even more likely to remember poems they create themselves.

Poetry (cont.)

⯌ Juxtaposition

This strategy prompts students to find and collect words from a variety of sources and encourages placement of words and phrases in a variety of ways to reveal fresh language and insights. McKim and Steinbergh note that with word bowl poetry, "the very fact of manipulating the words, discarding some, trading others, adding what one needs for sense, can teach us something about selection and choice in making poems. Joining two or three words that normally don't appear together can make fresh images, charging them with new energy and excitement" (1992, 38).

This strategy allows students to work with descriptions of concepts to create poems that reveal relationships and ideas about science content in unique and enlightening language. Putting words together through juxtaposition allows students to boil scientific ideas down to their essence. Students will benefit from having a range of words available from which to draw as they investigate scientific concepts.

⯌ Structured Poems

There are many forms of poetry that are created within specified formats. The structure of a certain number of words and syllables or a given pattern of rhythm helps students plan and organize their writing about scientific concepts. JoAnne Growney (2009) notes, "Long traditions embrace the fourteen-line sonnet with its ten-syllable lines. Five-line limericks and seventeen-syllable haiku also are familiar forms. Moreover, patterns of accent and rhyme overlay the line and syllable counts for even more intricacy" (12). The possibilities are endless as students engage with different patterns and writing within a particular structure, enabling scientific concepts to be viewed through a new lens. Furthermore, Corie Herman (2003) suggests that the structured nature of these poems supports diverse students' ability to succeed in writing them.

Dialogue Poems

Model Lesson: Science in Two Voices

Model Lesson Overview

Students read a poem written for two voices and work in pairs to create their own dialogue poems about weather and climate. As they do so, they gain a deeper understanding of the similarities and differences between the two scientific concepts. Dialogue poems also prompt students to better differentiate between two concepts that are usually learned at the same time, and thus sometimes confused, such as weather and climate.

Standards

K–2

- Knows that short-term weather conditions can change daily, and weather patterns change over the seasons

- Knows setting, main characters, main events, sequence, narrator, and problems in stories

3–5

- Knows that water exists in the air in different forms and changes from one form to another through various processes

- Knows the defining characteristics and structural elements of a variety of literary genres

- Makes connections between characters or simple events in a literary work and people or events in his or her own life

6–8

- Knows ways in which clouds affect weather and climate

- Knows the defining features and structural elements of a variety of literary genres

- Makes connections between the motives of characters or the causes for complex events in texts and those in his or her own life

9–12

- Knows the major external and internal sources of energy on Earth

- Uses precise and descriptive language that clarifies and enhances ideas and supports different purposes

Dialogue Poems *(cont.)*

Materials

- *Dialogue Poem Examples* (pages 140–141, dialogueexamples.pdf)

- *Two Voices Poem Plan* (page 142, twovoicesplan.pdf)

- Voice recording technology (*optional*)

Preparation

Familiarize yourself with the two examples of dialogue poems provided in the *Dialogue Poem Examples* (pages 140–141) activity sheet. Note that either side of the poem is to be read by a different voice and the italicized lines are to be read by both voices.

Think about scientific ideas that are related to weather and climate but have different characteristics, such as rain and snow or conduction and convection. Focus on concepts that are most relevant to your grade level.

Brainstorm characteristics of these concepts in preparation for a discussion with students. Use the terms and phrases drawn from this process to create your own dialogue poem. This will allow you to foresee what your students may encounter and will help you maximize your own understanding of dialogue poems so you can best guide students with appropriate resources and with the process itself. Try reading your poem out loud with an audience to get a sense of how different voices affect the meaning of the poem. Additional suggestions are provided in the Specific Grade Level Ideas.

Procedure

1. Display one or both of the dialogue poems from the *Dialogue Poem Examples* (pages 140–141) activity sheet, or share your own poem. Have two students read the different parts of the poem aloud.

2. Ask students, "What do you notice about how this poem is written? How does the poem reveal contrasting ideas? Shared ideas? What do you notice about the quality of the spoken lines when they are read by both voices?"

3. As a class, brainstorm a list of what they know about weather and climate, and record the list for students to refer to throughout the lesson. Encourage students to use primary and secondary sources to draw out more ideas and language that might be woven into the poems.

4. Divide students into pairs. Allow each pair to choose two concepts for their dialogue poem from the brainstormed list. The two concepts should be different but related, such as condensation and precipitation.

Dialogue Poems *(cont.)*

5. Distribute the *Two Voices Poem Plan* (page 142) activity sheet to each pair and provide time for them to write their own dialogue poems. Circulate among students and use the Planning Questions to guide discussion. Encourage students to create an image or provide visual examples to further exemplify the concepts.

6. Allow time for students to practice performing their poems aloud in two voices. As students develop their poems, encourage them to consider the content and order of the concepts they have included, and to revise based on both content and on how the poem sounds when read aloud by two voices.

7. Invite students to audiotape their performances and listen and discuss afterwards. You can also share these poems on a class blog or with software that supports voice recording.

8. Have each pair present their poem to the class. Use the Questions for Discussion to guide discussion.

Planning Questions

- What words or phrases are associated with each idea?

- How do the perspectives differ?

- What ideas do the perspectives share?

- What could you write that the voices could read together?

- What powerful word choices will you use?

- How will you embed examples of the science within the poem?

- How can you illustrate the poem so that the differences between these concepts are exemplified?

Questions for Discussion

- How did writing the poem in two voices help you identify the similarities and differences between the scientific concepts?

- How did listening to two separate voices help you discern the scientific concept?

- What did you learn about writing and articulating ideas by writing your poems?

- What feedback could you give the teams of authors about their poems?

Dialogue Poems *(cont.)*

Specific Grade Level Ideas

K–2

Students can draw from a brainstormed list of ideas about different but related observable scientific concepts such as rain and snow or liquid and solid. As a class, brainstorm a list of descriptive words. Students are likely to focus on examples based on what they see, hear, smell, and touch. Working together to articulate what they perceive with their senses can help clarify scientific concepts. For the youngest of students, the poem can be created as a whole-class activity. Possible topics for this strategy can include rocks and soils, the sun and the moon, or plants and animals.

3–5

Students can work with a partner on their dialogue poem after a group brainstorming session that clarifies the concepts and provides many language possibilities. In addition to working with weather and climate, this strategy can be used to explore related concepts such as night and day, rotation and revolution, survival and reproduction, or photosynthesis and respiration.

6–8

Students can focus on the connections and distinctions between weather and climate. Students can do some guided research to investigate the differences and connections and pull language from scientific texts. If writing over time, students can use an online file sharing service for their collaboration. Students can also consider more complex concepts that require some research and background information such as air and atmosphere, glaciers and icebergs, or eras and eons.

9–12

Students can investigate the difference between internal and external energy sources that affect weather and climate. Students can do their own research about the topic and can also do research and identify other factors of weather and climate that are related but need to be differentiated. Students can also use collaborative media, such as wikis, blogs, and file sharing, to integrate their research and develop the poem over time. This strategy can also be used to explore any content that is related but needs to be differentiated, such as meiosis and mitosis.

Dialogue Poem Examples

Tornado versus Hurricane
by David Williams

I was born

On the Great Plains

In the mid-Atlantic

I grew strong

As fronts clashed
Along the Dry Line,
Fueling the formation
Of cumulonimbus clouds

As warm air
Above the equatorial ocean
Created low pressure—
A tropical disturbance

I took form

As a supercell developed,
Generating hail and rain,
Slowly forming a swirling updraft:
A mesocyclone

As a cyclone developed,
Churning counterclockwise,
Gaining intensity:
A tropical storm

I earned my name

As a funnel cloud touched down,
Rotating faster and faster
A deadly vortex
Unpredictable

As my winds grew faster,
Over 75 miles per hour
A huge storm now
Capable of immense damage

Dialogue Poem Examples *(cont.)*

A force to be reckoned with

Measured

Tracked

Quantified on the Fujita scale

Rated on the Saffir-Simpson scale

I lived but a short time

Minutes or hours...

A few days or weeks...

Energy dissipated
And I ceased to be...

A tornado.

A hurricane.

Name _____ Date _____

Two Voices Poem Plan

Directions: Use this planning sheet to brainstorm ideas for your poem. Be sure to consider how the concepts are similar and different.

Concept: _____

Poem Title: _____

Voice 1
Words and Phrases:

_____

_____

_____

_____

Voice 2
Words and Phrases:

_____

_____

_____

_____

Combined Voices
Words and Phrases:

_____

_____

_____

_____

Bio Poems

Model Lesson: Where I'm from Scientifically

Model Lesson Overview

This particular approach to a bio poem is called an "I Am From" poem. "I Am From" poems were developed by teacher and writer George Ella Lyon (2010) and suggest a simple writing prompt for exploring personal histories. An adapted format is used here for exploring scientific bio poems. Students begin each line with the phrase *I am from* and then introduce specific details of their scientific histories. The reflective process provides both students and teachers with the opportunity to find connections among students' past experiences, to note how they solve science problems and learn best, and to recognize biases they may bring to the learning of science.

Standards

K–2

- Knows that in science it is helpful to work with a team and share findings with others

- Uses writing and other methods to describe familiar persons, places, objects, or experiences

3–5

- Knows that scientists' explanations about what happens in the world come partly from what they observe (evidence), and partly from how they interpret (inference) their observations

- Writes autobiographical compositions

- Writes narrative accounts, such as poems and stories

6–8

- Knows that the work of science requires a variety of human abilities, qualities, and habits of mind (e.g., reasoning, insight, energy, skill, creativity, intellectual honesty, tolerance of ambiguity, skepticism, openness to new ideas)

- Writes compositions about autobiographical incidents

Materials

- *Where I'm from Scientifically Examples* (page 147, wherefromexamples.pdf)

- *Where I'm from Scientifically Planner* (page 148, wherefromplanner.pdf)

Bio Poems *(cont.)*

Preparation

Read the *Where I'm from Scientifically Examples* (page 147) to become familiar with how the format can be used to write a scientific autobiography or science bio poem. You may also wish to write a "Where I'm from Scientifically" poem yourself to share with students. Additional suggestions are provided in the Specific Grade Level Ideas.

Procedure

1. Introduce the notion of being "from" someplace. Have students tell how they would respond to someone who asks casually, "Where are you from?" Then, have them discuss what would be different if a good friend asked, "So how did you get to be you? What things in your life shaped or influenced you?"

2. Using the prompt "What and where is science?," have students consider their scientific learning as you brainstorm a class list about science. Encourage students to extend their thinking to the many forms that science can take and the many dimensions of scientific concepts that play out in their lives. Have students consider science concepts, history, ideas, and processes. This will allow you to get a sense of what your students understand about science, even as you expand on their ideas of what and where science may be.

3. Explain to students that they are going to write their own scientific biographies as they relate to science. Ask them about the many ways they learn about science, including school, home, movies, books, people in their lives, etc.

4. Read aloud a bio poem from the *Where I'm from Scientifically Examples* (page 147) activity sheet, and have students discuss the ways in which the author describes his or her scientific experiences.

5. Distribute the *Where I'm from Scientifically Planner* (page 148) activity sheet, and have students discuss the various categories and possible responses. For example, they may think about their parents' attitudes toward science, their interests in science, or their expectations for learning science. You may also review the poem you read earlier in relation to the *Where I'm from Scientifically Planner*.

6. Allow time for students to reflect and record words, phrases, or sentences about their scientific memories.

7. Have students use their brainstormed words and phrases to create their own "Where I'm from Scientifically" poems. Be sure that students understand they don't have to include all of the topics or all of the words they brainstormed. Circulate among students, and use the Planning Questions to guide students' work.

Bio Poems *(cont.)*

8. Provide time for students to edit or confer about their poems in pairs and practice presenting their poems orally to one another.

9. Have students share their poems with the class. Use the Questions for Discussion to lead discussion about the poems.

Planning Questions

- What are some details about this scientific moment in your life?

- What are some other words that would help us understand how you felt about science while growing up?

- Was there a teacher who influenced you scientifically? If so, how?

- Are there stories in your life that relate to science?

- Can you include descriptions of scientific moments in your life that make us feel as if we are there?

- Which poetic devices can you use (e.g., repetition, metaphor, alliteration)?

Questions for Discussion

- How does this kind of poem help you learn about yourself?

- How might this kind of poem help you articulate your experience to others?

- What did you learn about the relationship of science to your life?

- What are some ways our poems are different? The same?

- What are some examples of words or phrases that helped us to understand another person's experiences?

- What do our poems suggest about how we learn to think about science?

Bio Poems *(cont.)*

Specific Grade Level Ideas

K–2

Students are likely learning about physical objects and exploration. Encourage them to also recognize that observation and experimentation are relevant to scientific learning. If possible, observe and record students' thinking as they develop their poems. Encourage younger students to draw pictures of scientific events rather than write about them, inviting them to develop spoken poems. You may be surprised to learn that even these young students often have clear views of themselves as learners of science.

3–5

Students can interview one another to complete the *Where I'm from Scientifically Planner* activity sheet. They can imagine that they are reporters trying to get the real story of their classmates' scientific lives and brainstorm additional questions to draw out scientific biographies. Students can interview family and friends outside of school and recall movies or TV shows they have watched and books they have read that include scientists or scientific ideas in one way or another.

6–8

Students will likely have several classroom memories they can draw from. Invite them to brainstorm and describe specific incidents, but ask that they do not mention teachers' names. Encourage students to probe the thinking of several members of their family and to become sensitive to the ways in which science is portrayed in the media or by teachers of other subjects.

Students can take on the persona of a scientific concept and write a bio poem from that perspective, such as "I am an organelle…."

Where I'm from Scientifically Examples

Grades K–2

I am from the buggy place
Ants crawl along the cracks in the sidewalk
I watch them build their homes and carry their food
I like to see the moon at night
I am from the earth
I am a scientist

—by Gene Diaz

Grades 3–5

Geologist

I am from samples of rocks and minerals,
Categorizing, sorting, classifying,
Streak, light, luster,
Minerals reveal their properties.

I am from magma, sediment, heat, and pressure.
I am from studying the forces that shape the Earth.
I am a geologist.

—by Brittany Williams

Grades 6–8

I am from a father who is an engineer and a mother who loves to cook.
He says, "$E = mc^2$," and she says, "Isn't this yummy?"
I am from building projects with cardboard and kicking soccer balls,
I am from the land of cartoons and make-believe,
And goals and goals and goals.
I am from "Why does this work?" and "Tell how you know."
I am from making diagrams and building models.
I am from doing experiments outdoors working in groups,
Water, soil, erosion on the earth.
I am from feeling good when I understand how to take care of the planet.

—by Gene Diaz

Name _____   Date _____

Where I'm from Scientifically Planner

Directions: Fill in the boxes to brainstorm ideas for a "Where I'm from Scientifically" poem. Then, on a separate sheet of paper, write your poem, beginning some lines with *I am from….*

My parents and science:	What I do in my free time and science:
What words or quotes I have heard about science:	My friends and science:
How I solve science problems:	How I learn science best:

Rhyme and Rhythm

Model Lesson: Concept Rhymes

Model Lesson Overview

In this lesson, students explore the rhyme and meter of different poems about science by reading them aloud with expression. They discuss how performing poetry relies on working with the rhythm and meter of a poem. Students investigate syllables and patterns by reading aloud, playing with volume, pace, rhythm, intonation, and proper pronunciation as they bring ideas in the poem to life. Students also share their thoughts about rhyming and nonrhyming poems. Finally, students perform their favorite poems again and again, allowing them to internalize concepts in the poems.

Standards

K-2

- Knows that living things go through a process of growth and change

- Writes in a variety of forms or genres

3-5

- Knows that living organisms have distinct structures and body systems that serve specific functions in growth, survival, and reproduction

- Knows the defining characteristics and structural elements of a variety of literary genres

6-8

- Knows that waves have energy and interact with matter and can transfer energy

- Uses content, style, and structure appropriate for specific audiences and purposes

9-12

- Uses strategies to adapt writing for different purposes

- Writes descriptive compositions

Rhyme and Rhythm *(cont.)*

Materials

- Poetry books with rhyming and nonrhyming poems
- Audio-recording software (*optional*)
- *Science Concept Poem Examples* (page 153, scienceconcept.pdf)
- *Rhymes and Rhythms Planning Guide* (page 154, rhymesrhythm.pdf)
- *My Science Concept Poem* (page 155, mysccienceconcept.pdf)

Preparation

Gather both rhyming and nonrhyming poems. Have different poetry books available so that students can choose poems of interest. If desired, have audio-recording software available for students to record and rerecord their recitations. Think about how scientific information is conceptualized and how possible misconceptions may be related. Reflect on scientific data to aid in identifying the concepts that you want students to focus on, or, if appropriate, have students identify the concepts that they want to understand in more depth. Begin by thinking about how systems are often described by scientists in relation to their functions in an organism (circulatory, respiratory, etc.), and think of the other ways systems are often described (by location, by the key components, etc.). Identify examples of humorous poems that rhyme and that students will enjoy. Locate at least two poems with different rhyme schemes. Some poems are suggested in the Specific Grade Level Ideas. Review the sample poems in the *Science Concept Poem Examples* (page 153) activity sheet. Share these with students as models or create examples of your own.

Procedure

1. Read aloud a poem from the *Science Concept Poem Examples* (page 153), or read your selected example. As you read the poem, ask students to pay particular attention to the rhyming words and rhythmic patterns they hear. Discuss the poem with students.

2. Display the poem for students to see and ask students to identify where the rhyming words occur in the stanzas. Have students identify the rhyme scheme. Repeat this process with a second poem so that students recognize that a variety of rhyming patterns are possible.

3. Divide students into pairs and distribute the *Rhymes and Rhythms Planning Guide* (page 154) activity sheet to each student. Have students work together to conduct research about a science concept. Encourage students to explore multiple related science concepts to deepen their understanding of a single concept before writing. Then, have students brainstorm rhyming words and rhythmic patterns that relate to the science concept, such as human body systems. Students should work together to gather ideas, but each student should record the ideas on their own sheet of paper.

Rhyme and Rhythm (cont.)

4. Tell students that they will independently write a poem using the rhyming words and/or rhythms they recorded. Distribute the *My Science Concept Poem* (page 155) activity sheet to students. Provide time for students to create, edit, and illustrate their poems. Circulate among students as they work and use the Planning Questions to stimulate students' thinking.

5. Provide time for students to practice reading their poems aloud with rhythm and intonation. Have students read their poems aloud to the class. Post students' poems in the classroom for them to refer to later, thus increasing the likelihood of understanding and recall.

6. Use the Questions for Discussion to debrief the activity.

Planning Questions

- What scientific ideas will you include in your poem?

- How might you incorporate rhyme?

- How might you incorporate rhythm?

- How will you work to match the rhythm of the syllables in each line?

- What image(s) will you use to illustrate your concept poem?

Questions for Discussion

- What elements created the patterns (syllables, alliteration, onomatopoeia, etc.)?

- What sensory details brought the poem to life?

- What metaphors and/or similes were effective?

Specific Grade Level Ideas

K–2

"The Drinking Fountain" by Marchette Chute or "The Secret Place" by Tomie dePaola are good poems to introduce this activity. Students can write poems about simple concepts, such as grouping organisms (plants, animals, nonliving objects) or the life cycles of different organisms. Their rhymes are likely to be exact rhymes of one-syllable words, such as *plant* or *leaf*. By sound, they will be able to recognize words that sound but are not spelled the same, such as *plant* and *ant*. You may want students to have the alphabet at hand to organize their thinking about possible rhymes. A standard format of the first line will make it easier for students to create their own examples.

Rhyme and Rhythm *(cont.)*

3–5

"Messy Room" by Shel Silverstein and "Children's Party" by Ogden Nash are good poems to introduce this activity. The book *The Beauty of the Beast: Poems from the Animal Kingdom* by Jack Prelutsky contains poems organized by biological classification categories. Students can write poems about concepts that require memorization, such as the phases of the water cycle. You can introduce the notion of two-syllable rhymes as well as near- or half-rhymes, such as *phylum* and *happen*. These are also called *slant rhymes*.

6–8

Introduce the activity with a more sophisticated poem, such as "The Cloud" by Percy Shelley. Students can create poems that show a sophisticated understanding of human body systems or other concepts, such as Earth systems (layers of the atmosphere, factors that impact the climate, tilt of Earth's axis and seasons) or properties of matter (molecular arrangement and motion, chemical reactions). Students can create rhythmic poems using mnemonic devices to help them remember the periodic table or the seven categories of biological taxonomy (**K**ingdom **P**hylum **C**lass **O**rder **F**amily **G**enus **S**pecies).

9–12

Students can write poems about the Periodic Table of the Elements in order to commit important information about the elements to memory. For example, students could write poems that explore the characteristics of noble gases or halogens, noting the similarities and differences the elements share in the structure of a rhyming and/or rhythmic poem. Students could also use this strategy to delve into the different ionic and covalent bonds, using rhyme and rhythm as a vehicle for comparing the similarities, the differences, the respective strengths and weaknesses of either bond, and the respective stability of either bond.

Science Concept Poem Examples

Grades K–2

The Butterfly

He eats and eats and eats and eats
And spins into a chrysalis
From caterpillar to winged delight
An amazing metamorphosis

Grades 3–5

Who Knew?

In science today,
I realized I
rely upon alveoli
inside my lungs
where millions live,
an amazing contribution
to life they give,
these little hollow cavities
at the terminal end
of the respiratory tree
where pumping blood
by sacs will pass
and on the way
exchange gas.
CO_2 leaves through diffusion,
absorbing oxygen,
reducing confusion!
Ah, the structure of anatomy.

Grades 6–8

Flashbulb

Flash!
Reflect, refract, absorb
Photo has an orb
blur of light
circle of white
light
bounces off solid particles
on my camera lens
light bends
can be a
cause for celebration
when there's a chromatic aberration

Grades 9–12

Earthquake

Tectonic plates shift
Seismographs record data:
Earthquake predicted.

Light and Sound

Light
Color, intensity
Reflecting, refracting, absorbing
Electromagnetic, visible, audible, kinetic
Absorbing, reflecting, vibrating
Pitch, volume
Sound

Name _____   Date _____

Rhymes and Rhythms Planning Guide

Directions: With your partner, conduct research about your science concept and record important words and/or rhythmic phrases you discover. Then, brainstorm interesting rhymes and/or rhythms you may want to include in your poem. You may also record words and phrases about related science concepts to help you.

Science Concept	Rhyming Words and/or Rhythmic Phrases
Interesting Word Rhymes	**Interesting Word Rhythms**

Name _____   Date _____

My Science Concept Poem

Directions: Use the space to write and illustrate your science concept poem.

Concept

Poem

Illustration

Juxtaposition

Model Lesson: Scientific Word Bowls

Model Lesson Overview

In this lesson, students brainstorm or read about words they associate with the engineering design process and then put the terms together in new ways to create poems that depict scientific understanding. Students are encouraged to experiment with a variety of ways of juxtaposing selected words and adding others as needed.

Standards

K–2

- Knows that planning is an important part of the design process
- Writes in a variety of forms or genres
- Uses descriptive words to convey basic ideas

3–5

- Knows that group collaboration is useful as the combination of multiple creative minds can yield more possible design solutions
- Uses a variety of sentence structures in writing
- Uses descriptive and precise language that clarifies and enhances ideas

6–8

- Knows that the design process relies on different strategies: creative brainstorming to establish many design solutions, evaluating the feasibility of various solutions in order to choose a design, and troubleshooting the selected design
- Uses a variety of sentence structures to expand and embed ideas
- Uses descriptive language that clarifies and enhances ideas
- Analyzes how a drama's or poem's form or structure contributes to its meaning

Materials

- *Poetry Word List* (page 160, poetrywordlist.pdf)
- Reusable containers or shoeboxes
- Scissors
- Microphone (*optional*)

Juxtaposition *(cont.)*

Preparation

Create a list of engineering design concepts that students are familiar with but could deepen their understanding about, such as observation, measurement, construction, testing, design, problem solving, research, modeling, improvement, materials, systems, solutions, teamwork, and sustainability.

Decide how to group students in teams of two or three. Prepare a chart with one of the scientific design concepts listed at the top.

Collect reusable containers or shoeboxes to serve as word bowls. Additional suggestions are provided in the Specific Grade Level Ideas.

Procedure

1. Have students brainstorm words that they associate with the chosen design concept. Record brainstormed words and phrases so students can refer to them throughout the lesson.

2. Ask students to help you create a class poem by selecting words and phrases from the list and arranging them into a poem. The idea is to put the words together and play with the line breaks in a variety of ways until a clear sense of the idea being explored is established. Encourage metaphors, similes, and the use of imagery, sensory descriptors, and feeling words.

3. Divide students into small groups and assign groups an engineering design concept. Distribute the *Poetry Word List* (page 160) activity sheet to each group, and have students collect words and short phrases from research materials and textbooks for powerful words and phrases to add to their lists.

4. Distribute a box, a bowl, or another container to each group to serve as a word bowl. Have students cut their words apart and place them in the word bowl.

5. Ask students to take a few words from the bowl and then work together to juxtapose the words in different ways. Remind them to pay careful attention to how the arrangement impacts meaning. Tell groups that the selected words and phrases are just a starting point to spark ideas. They can choose to not use certain words, they can draw additional words from the bowl, or they can add words and phrases they prefer.

6. Once their poems are complete, each group should write out a final version to share with the class. Students can also add images and numbers to illustrate the ideas.

7. Allow time for students to rehearse reading their poems aloud chorally to bring them to life.

Juxtaposition (cont.)

8. If desired, plan a poetry slam where students present their poems to a larger audience. Have students read their poems to the class. If available, bring in a microphone and invite other classes to hear the poems.

9. Use the Questions for Discussion to debrief the class.

Questions for Discussion

- Why is it important to describe engineering design ideas in words?

- What did you learn through the process of creating a poem?

- What unique or fresh language came out of the exploration of juxtaposing different words and phrases?

- What did you learn from listening to the poems of others?

- How did you use artistic, expressive language to discuss and better understand science concepts?

Specific Grade Level Ideas

K–2

Students should work in small groups with you. They can brainstorm fewer words without reference to parts of speech. Poetry themes can include language related to materials and tools. Students can also address solutions, using known materials and tools for new designs and solutions.

This strategy can be used to reinforce learning about the biological world, such as seeds and plants, or physical concepts, such as weight and height.

3–5

Possible themes for poems include materials, time, tools, safety, scientific laws, engineering principles, and environmental impact.

This strategy can also be used to explore other scientific concepts, such as celestial bodies, rock formations, or the seasons.

Juxtaposition (cont.)

6–8

After exploring the task as a whole class and assigning each group their design concept, students can create their initial list of words for homework using the *Poetry Word List* activity sheet. Then, provide time for students to combine their ideas at the end of the week. These combinations should demonstrate good planning and design so that the poems fit together in a way that makes sense. You may also wish students to make copies of their first drafts as well as their final poems, along with individual reflections on the process. Students should be expected to produce descriptive language. Examples of themes include model, systems, acceptability, suitability, sustainability, quality, modifications, etc.

Name _____ Date _____

Poetry Word List

Directions: Record words and short phrases about your topic in the spaces below. Then, cut out the words and place them in the word bowl. Draw out a few words and arrange them in different ways. Play with the arrangement of these words and phrases to create meaning, mood, and rhythm.

My collection of words and phrases:

Structured Poems

Model Lesson: Cinquain

Model Lesson Overview

The cinquain structure guides the development of a poem by inviting the writer to use a prescribed sequence of words, types of words, or syllables in each line. Students write cinquain poems as they note the patterns in the structure and reflect on scientific concepts and vocabulary.

Standards

K–2

- Knows that heat can be produced in many ways (e.g., burning, rubbing, mixing substances together)
- Writes in a variety of forms or genres
- Uses adjectives in written composition

3–5

- Knows that heat is often produced as a byproduct when one form of energy is converted to another form (e.g., when machines and living organisms convert stored energy to motion)
- Knows the defining characteristics and structural elements of a variety of literary genres
- Uses a variety of sentence structures in writing

6–8

- Knows that energy is a property of many substances (e.g., heat energy is in the disorderly motion of molecules and in radiation; chemical energy is in the arrangement of atoms; mechanical energy is in moving bodies or in elastically distorted shapes; electrical energy is in the attraction or repulsion between charges)
- Uses precise and descriptive language that clarifies and enhances ideas and supports different purposes
- Uses a variety of sentence structures and lengths

Structured Poems (cont.)

Materials

- *Cinquain Examples* (page 165, cinquainexamples.pdf)
- *Word-Count Cinquain Planner* (page 166, cinquainplanner1.pdf)
- *Parts of Speech Cinquain Planner* (page 167, cinquainplanner2.pdf)
- *Syllables Cinquain Planner* (page 168, cinquainplanner3.pdf)

Preparation

Try writing a cinquain poem to experience working within the structures prescribed in the *Word-Count Cinquain Planner* (page 166), the *Parts of Speech Cinquain Planner* (page 167), and the *Syllables Cinquain Planner* (page 168) activity sheets. Reflect on the criteria of the poems that you find easiest to meet and those you found most challenging. Additional suggestions are provided in the Specific Grade Level Ideas.

Procedure

1. Display the *Cinquain Examples* (page 165) activity sheet, or share cinquains of your own creation. Read the poems aloud to students, have students read along with you, or ask student volunteers to read the poems aloud. Then, read the poems to students again, asking listeners to consider the rhythm, word choices, and mood, and to identify how the poem brings a scientific idea to life.

2. Ask, "What do you notice about how these poems bring scientific ideas to life? What do you learn about each concept? How are these poems alike?" Allow time for students to identify ideas related to the number of lines, the number of words in each line, the types of words in each line, the scientific theme, and the shape of the poems.

3. As a class, select a scientific concept about which to write a class cinquain poem. Then, collectively identify a term for the first line of the poem. Invite students to brainstorm additional words associated with this concept. Suggested terms and concepts to use for the first line of the poems are listed in the Specific Grade Level Ideas. You can also refer students to a science word wall if you have one in your classroom.

4. Display the *Word-Count Cinquain Planner* (page 166), the *Parts of Speech Cinquain Planner* (page 167), or the *Syllables Cinquain Planner* (page 168) activity sheet, whichever is most appropriate for students. As a class, work through ideas for the different lines of the class poem, drawing from the list of brainstormed words.

Structured Poems *(cont.)*

5. Divide students into small groups, and have each group create a cinquain poem, either by building on the ideas generated as a class or by creating a new poem on a different scientific topic. Circulate among the groups and use the Planning Questions to help students visualize images and use their senses. Note that these poem structures are not meant to be formulaic but rather as structures to spark creativity. The cinquain structure prompts students to make careful choices about how best to represent ideas and distill their thinking.

6. Have each group read its cinquain poem aloud to the class. Use the Questions for Discussion to debrief the activity.

Planning Questions

- What word will you choose to start your poem? What related word will you use for the last line?

- Close your eyes and think about your word. What do you see? What do you feel? What does this word remind you of? Which words on the list do you like best?

- What actions can you brainstorm that connect to your word? Which action words give new insights about the scientific ideas?

- What feelings do you associate with this scientific term?

Questions for Discussion

- What choices did you make as you selected words and phrases for your poem?

- What did you learn from the poems read by other members of our class?

- What language was most compelling?

- How did the sound and rhythm of the poems help communicate meaning?

- What are the main ideas communicated about each topic?

- How does writing a poem compare to sharing ideas in essays or book chapters?

Structured Poems *(cont.)*

Specific Grade Level Ideas

K–2

It will be easiest for students to focus on the number of words in each line of a cinquain while using the *Word-Count Cinquain Planner* activity sheet.

Possible words for the first line include general terms describing heat (hot, mixing, burning, rubbing, energy), heat produced by burning (fire, wood, coal, sun, light, ash), or heat produced by rubbing things together (friction, movement, hands, warm). Students may also use particular ideas about heat that are relevant to them, such as a fireplace, a campfire, or a candle.

This strategy can be used to explore other scientific topics such as weather (rain, snow, water cycle), living organisms (animal, plant, needs, ecosystem), or energy (sun, electricity, sound, light).

3–5

Students can use the *Word-Count Cinquain Planner* or the *Parts of Speech Cinquain Planner* activity sheet.

Possible words for the first line include ways that heat is produced when living organisms convert stored energy to motion (breathe, run, swim, sprout, grow, bloom), heat that is produced when machines convert stored energy to motion (kinetic, engine, motor, turbine, noise, spark, gears), heat that moves from one object to another by conduction (transfer, flow, gradient, thermal, diffusion), or properties associated with heat conductivity (insulation, thermal, conductivity, coefficient, resistivity).

This strategy can be used to explore other topics such as the water cycle, the composition of the earth, or plant structure and growth.

6–8

Have students use the *Syllables Cinquain Planner* activity sheet. Have students consider the concept of energy as a property of many substances, such as heat, mechanical, electrical, or chemical, for possible first lines.

Cinquain Examples

Word-Count Cinquain

Hot

Fire, flames

Burning, crackling, glowing

Warmth from the hearth,

Heat

Parts of Speech Cinquain

Mobile

Quickly moving

Rolling, rumbling, rambling, rusting,

Burning dirty fossil fuels

Auto

Syllable Cinquain

Energy moves

Transforms and transfers

Powerful changes shape lives

Wind turbines turn

Turn, turn

Name _____   Date _____

Word-Count Cinquain Planner

Directions: Collect words about your topic of study. Then, use the structure to create a meaningful cinquain poem. Experiment with different word choices.

Topic for my poem: _____

_____

Word collection: _____

_____

_____

My poem:

Title: _____

One word: _____

Two words: _____ _____

Three words: _____ _____ _____

Four words: _____ _____ _____ _____

One word: _____

Name _____ Date _____

Parts of Speech Cinquain Planner

Directions: Collect words about your topic of study. Then, use the structure to create a meaningful cinquain poem. Experiment with different word choices.

Topic for my poem: _____

_____

Word collection: _____

_____

_____

My poem:

Title: _____

Adjectives: _____   _____

-ing words: _____   _____   _____

Phrase: _____   _____   _____   _____

Synonym for title word: _____

Name _____   Date _____

Syllables Cinquain Planner

Directions: Collect words about your topic of study. Then, use the structure to create a meaningful cinquain poem. Experiment with different word choices.

Topic for my poem: _____

_____

Word collection: _____

_____

_____

My poem:

Title: _____

Two syllables: _____ _____

Four syllables: _____ _____ _____ _____

Six syllables: _____ _____ _____ _____ _____ _____

Eight syllables: _____ _____ _____ _____ _____ _____ _____ _____

Two syllables: _____ _____

Storytelling

Storytelling

Understanding Storytelling

Storytelling has been part of every culture since the beginning of time (Norfolk, Stenson, and Williams 2006). Stories have been used to educate, to inspire, and to entertain. There is the story itself, and there is the telling of the tale by a skilled teller. Storytellers use language, gesture, eye contact, tone, and inflection as they share a story with an audience. A good storyteller can create a sense of instant community among listeners as well as a deep connection with the material being explored (Hamilton and Weiss 2005). Because the storyteller interacts with the audience as the story is told, listeners often feel that they become part of the story world. They can even feel as if they are co-creators of the story when it is interactive, when connections with characters are developed, and when empathy is established. If you've ever heard a good storyteller tell a compelling story, you know it can transport you to another time and place.

In the following strategies, students benefit both from listening to stories and from becoming storytellers themselves. As listeners, students are supported in their visualization of the stories, which makes a narrative easier to both imagine and remember (Donovan and Pascale 2012). As storytellers, students develop additional skills, including skilled use of voice, improved verbal and nonverbal communication skills, and sense of pacing. Once stories are developed, you can also ask students to write them down, further enhancing their literacy skills.

When your students become storytellers, they fine-tune their communication skills. Oral fluency is developed as they explore vocal tone and inflection, pacing, sound effects, and the addition of rich sensory details to the telling. Listeners feel invited on a journey. Also, participating in the creation and telling of stories brings forward students' voices and their ideas.

Scientific ideas are easily embedded in or teased out of stories. Students find that stories provide vivid contexts that show the relevance and use of scientific thinking. Well-placed scientific problems can easily be connected to characters' dilemmas, requiring solutions in order for the story to advance. Such dilemmas can provide additional points of interaction for students and heighten the dramatic tension of the story.

As students create, tell, and retell stories, they are gaining fluency in their communication skills, use of descriptive language, and persuasive abilities. They are also expanding their willingness to revisit, revise, and polish their work. By placing the sciences in story settings, we provide a context that gives further meaning to the scientific ideas and adds interest to the stories.

Storytelling (cont.)

Strategies for Storytelling

ᴃᴏ Prompt

Students are invited to become storytellers themselves as they brainstorm, develop, and perform stories from a given prompt. In this strategy, an interview is used as a prompt. Students conduct an interview as a starting point and then weave a story, using what they learned. Students are charged with finding a way for the story to unfold and are in control of its progression. This strategy works to develop many skills—understanding of beginning, middle, and end; character development; and the significance of circumstance, setting, and mood in creating compelling stories that are performed and engage the listener.

ᴃᴏ Personification

Some people only use *personification* to refer to when we assign human qualities to inanimate objects or ideas and use the term *anthropomorphism* when we assign human qualities to animals. Other folks use these terms interchangeably. We will use *personification* to refer to all such assignment of human characteristics as it is most familiar to teachers and students, but feel free to use what best fits your curriculum. Personification is an ancient storytelling tool that continues today; think of both Aesop's Fables and the Toy Story movies (Cahill 2006). Stories that give animals and objects human traits allow listeners to think about their shortcomings in a safe way and invite us to think about moral or ethical values. These tales engage learners and allow us to consider different perspectives. Because animals and objects take on human characteristics, the strategy also lends itself to figurative language.

ᴃᴏ Points of Entry

Entering at different points of the story can provide different structures for building a narrative. We have prequels that start before stories, we can add a new segment to the middle of a story, and in daily life, we sometimes work backward to figure out where we need to begin. These different points of entry provide a frame that can support students' abilities to create a story as well as to gain a deeper understanding of cause-and-effect relationships. In creating such stories, students analyze, evaluate, and create, the three highest-order thinking skills in Benjamin Bloom's revised taxonomy (Anderson et al. 2000).

Storytelling *(cont.)*

∞ Retelling

Storytelling is an oral tradition that is grounded in telling and retelling stories. With each retelling, a story grows more polished, more dramatic, with clear high points and striking moments, building interest and engaging denouements as students experiment with variations in every sharing. They become more responsive to working with their listeners and more adept at using the storytelling process to spark the imagination of the audience. This revisiting of stories also strengthens students' writing skills as stories get honed and more richly detailed with each retelling. Additionally, retelling also strengthens students' scientific understanding as they add rich details based on their scientific understanding of what is being represented in the story.

∞ Collaborative Storytelling

Collaborative storytelling often takes place in kids' play (Hourcade et al. 2003) and has been part of the cultural traditions of many families and communities (Coulter, Michael, and Poynor 2007). In this strategy, students work together to build a story by adding short segments in their oral telling. Stories can be sparked by graphics, character traits, or settings. The story can be "passed" back and forth with each teller adding details and information before passing it on. A natural part of the process is a series of unexpected twists and turns that challenge students to maintain a shared strand, keeping a clear logic so that the story remains together as it unfolds. This challenges them to listen attentively to the details and story choices so that they can build on the unfolding events in meaningful and compelling ways by pivoting off details given, such as character traits, circumstance, and action. Students introduce obstacles and innovative solutions that take the characters on surprising journeys. Jude Yew (2005) notes that constructing knowledge through the collective creation of narratives can provide more effective ways of learning in group settings than learning concepts individually.

Prompt

Model Lesson: Invent a Scientist

Model Lesson Overview

Students gather primary source information as they interview scientists to find out what they do, what teams they work with, and what problems they have solved with their teams. Students use these problems as prompts to create and tell a story about an imaginary team of scientists solving a scientific problem. Students share their ideas about what a scientist is, use inquiry and research strategies to find out what scientists do, and use their imaginations to create a story in which the characters solve a scientific problem as a team.

Standards

K–2

- Knows that students can do science
- Knows that in science it is helpful to work with a team and share findings with others
- Knows setting, main characters, main events, sequence, narrator, and problems in stories

3–5

- Knows that people of all ages, backgrounds, and groups have made contributions to science and technology throughout history
- Knows that scientists and engineers often work in teams to accomplish a task
- Understands elements of character development in literary works
- Organizes ideas for oral presentations

6–8

- Knows that people of all backgrounds and with diverse interests, talents, qualities, and motivations engage in fields of science and engineering; some of these people work in teams and others work alone, but all communicate extensively with others
- Knows that the work of science requires a variety of human abilities, qualities, and habits of mind (e.g., reasoning, insight, energy, skill, creativity, intellectual honesty, tolerance of ambiguity, skepticism, openness to new ideas)
- Knows various settings in which scientists and engineers may work
- Understands elements of character development in literary works

Prompt *(cont.)*

Materials

- Images of scientists

- *Scientist Interview* (page 178, scientistinterview.pdf)

- *Story Planning Questions* (page 179, storyquestions.pdf)

Preparation

Locate local or accessible scientists either in your community, in your networks, or on the Internet. You can find and make connections to scientists by searching "find a scientist" online. The NISE Network (http://nisenet.org/) can connect you with nanoscientists in your area who are interested in collaborating with schools and serving as content advisors. Additionally, the Philadelphia Science Festival (http://www.philasciencefestival.org/) has a feature on its website where both scientists and teachers can sign up to connect. You can also contact nearby universities, and, most importantly, you can ask students and others in your community if they know of any scientists who would serve as resources for the work required of students in this lesson.

Gather a variety of images of scientists to share with students. Conduct an Internet search for images of scientists. These images will serve as the foundation for a conversation about who scientists are and what they do. Additional suggestions are provided in the Specific Grade Level Ideas.

Procedure

1. Ask students what they know about science, asking questions such as, "What is science? Have you read stories or seen movies about scientists? Do you know any scientists? Share images of scientists in a variety of settings and continue to expand on your questions, asking, "Who is a scientist? Where do scientists work and what do they do? What kinds of teams do they work with?" Brainstorm and record a list of as many kinds of scientists as you and your students can think of.

2. Tell students that they will interview scientists about the work they do. Ask them how you as a class can find scientists to interview. Take their suggestions and be sure to add your own if they do not include all viable resources.

3. Divide students into groups of 3 and have each group identify a scientist to research. Tell them that they can do some research on the Internet, but they need to also interview their scientist, either in person, on the phone, or over the Internet.

Prompt *(cont.)*

4. Distribute the *Scientist Interview* (page 178) activity sheet to each student group. For practice, ask students to think about a time when they solved a problem with a team. Have them interview one another about their experience. Ask them to record their data and share with the class what they learned about their interview partner.

5. With your assistance or independently, have students contact their scientist and conduct an interview, depending on age and access. If the scientist is local, students could invite him or her to class to meet in person. Otherwise, students can conduct their interviews online or over the phone.

6. Have students share their data with the class. Ask questions such as, "What kinds of problems did you learn about? Where do your scientists do their work? Who else is involved in the work?"

7. Tell students that they will use what they learned from the interviews to create a story about an imaginary team of scientists solving a problem. Ask each student to think of a scientific problem they want their story to be about. This will be the prompt on which they will base their story. Review the elements of storytelling, such as *character*, *setting*, *plot*, *action*, *dialogue*, or any other relevant elements. Then, identify a particular issue that the scientist had to wrestle with and how he or she worked to resolve it.

8. Distribute the *Story Planning Questions* (page 179) activity sheet to students, and direct them to answer the questions and use their answers to develop a story about their imaginary team of scientists. Remind students to use voice and gesture to personify each scientist in the team.

9. Provide time for students to work on their stories and practice telling them aloud to partners or small groups. They should use peer feedback to improve their stories and storytelling.

10. Have students share their final stories with the whole class. Use the Questions for Discussion to review and debrief.

Questions for Discussion

- What did you need to know about science, scientists, and storytelling to develop a believable story?

- How did you decide what kind of scientists would be part of your team?

- How did you translate your research into the elements of a story, including character, setting, dialogue, and unfolding action?

- How did you use voice and gestures to tell the story?

- How did telling your story support your understanding of what scientists do?

Prompt (cont.)

Specific Grade Level Ideas

K–2

Invite one or more scientists to visit your classroom. Prepare interview questions by brainstorming with students. What would they like to know about the scientist's work and those he or she works with? Have students practice asking questions of you or another adult to practice how they will act when the scientist comes. You could also use the questions students brainstormed to interview scientists online. As a class, talk about the kinds of problems scientists solve with help from others and develop a story together.

3–5

Have students look at construction in your community (new tunnels, a new museum, a building under restoration) and create a story about a team of people working on the project. Students can explore local issues that require a team of experts from different disciplines to solve a problem (engineers, architects, scientists, etc.).

This strategy can be used to explore any science content by having students investigate and create stories about particular types of scientists and problems, ranging from engineering to environmental science to astronomy or medicine.

6–8

Have each group of students define a local problem and create a story about potential solutions, describing the team and the constraints that they would have to keep in mind when deciding on the solution. Be sure to also include an interesting contingency the team must overcome as they solve the problem. This will provide excitement in the development of the plot.

This strategy can be used to explore any number of problems in multiple areas of science and engineering as students can investigate local problems in health care, transportation, the environment, or any other scientific topic reflected in their local area.

Name _____   Date _____

Scientist Interview

Directions: Use the questions to interview a scientist. Be sure to read the questions in advance. Add any additional questions that seem relevant to your research.

1. What is your name? _____

2. What kind of work do you do and what kinds of problems do you work with?

   _____

   _____

3. What skills and habits do you need to have for your work?

   _____

   _____

4. Can you share a scientific problem you solved as a member of a team?

   _____

   _____

5. Can you tell me about who made up the team? What skills did they bring?

   _____

   _____

6. How did you resolve the problem?

   _____

   _____

7. How did your team share its findings?

   _____

   _____

Name _____   Date _____

Story Planning Questions

Directions: Answer the questions about your imaginary team of scientists and use your answers to develop and tell a story.

1. What problem will your team of scientists encounter?

   _____

   _____

2. Who will be on the team?

   _____

   _____

3. How will your team use their skills to solve that problem?

   _____

   _____

4. What will be the setting for the team's work?

   _____

   _____

5. How will the team resolve the problem?

   _____

   _____

6. How will the team share its findings?

   _____

   _____

Personification

Model Lesson: Keystone Species

Model Lesson Overview

In this strategy, students investigate the interconnected relationship of various animals to a keystone species as they tell a story from an animal's point of view. Personification allows students to consider new perspectives and explore difficult ethical and moral dilemmas.

Standards

K-2

- Knows that living things are found almost everywhere in the world and that distinct environments support the life of different types of plants and animals

- Selects interrelated characters, environments, and situations for simple dramatizations

- Uses level-appropriate vocabulary in speech

3-5

- Knows that changes in the environment can have different effects on different organisms

- Selects interrelated characters, environments, and situations for simple dramatizations

- Understands the importance of characters' actions to the plot and theme

6-8

- Knows the factors that affect the number of organisms an ecosystem can support

- Knows the factors that affect the types of organisms an ecosystem can support

- Understands elements of character development in literary works

Materials

- A book that outlines the life of a particular species and its place in an ecosystem

- *Fact Finding and Observations* (page 184, factfinding.pdf)

- *Concept Map 1* (conceptmap1.pdf) or *Concept Map 2* (conceptmap2.pdf)

- *Story Planner* (page 185, storyplanner.pdf)

Personification *(cont.)*

Preparation

Select a book that outlines the life of a particular species and its place in an ecosystem, such as *At Home with the Gopher Tortoise: The Story of a Keystone Species* by Madeleine Dunphy, or select other similar stories about symbiotic relationships within an ecosystem. Practice reading the book aloud, and as you read, think about how to personify each animal. Experiment with the animals' voices and gestures to make the story come alive. As you read the story, note the different relationships between animals and take note of the interdependence of species and how the balance of an ecosystem can be disrupted by the removal of a single species. Make a list of all the organisms in the ecosystem and decide how the animal names will be distributed to students. Additional suggestions are provided in the Specific Grade Level Ideas.

Procedure

1. Begin a conversation with students about interdependent relationships by asking questions such as, "What do humans need to survive? What do animals need? What would an animal's habitat include? How are animals dependent on other animals or plants?" If students overlook the basic survival needs, be sure to mention water, space, food sources, and shelter.

2. Assign animals from your selected story to students to personify. You may need to assign the same animal to more than one student. Distribute the *Fact Finding and Observations* (page 184) activity sheet for students to complete as you read the story aloud.

3. Read aloud your selected story about different types of independent relationships. Engage students as data collectors by asking students to listen for their assigned animals in the story and record characteristics of the animals (behavior, physical features, etc.) and how their animal relates to other organisms on the *Fact Finding and Observations* activity sheet. Stop reading occasionally to ask students to point out some of the relationships, such as which animals provide shelter or food for other animals. Ask students what makes a good story. Then, list story elements such as *character*, *setting*, *conflict*, *dialogue*, and *action* for students to reference throughout the lesson.

4. Ask students to discuss how the various species share interdependent relationships. Record students' observations in a concept map. See the *Concept Map 1* (conceptmap1.pdf) or *Concept Map 2* (conceptmap2.pdf) reference sheet on the Digital Resource CD for concept map samples, and display it for students to reference throughout the lesson.

5. After each student has shared how his or her species is connected to the web of relationships, present students with a scenario in which the keystone species is removed from the web. Discuss what would happen and which relationships would be affected both directly and indirectly.

Personification *(cont.)*

6. Group students together who have the same assigned animal and distribute one *Story Planner* (page 185) activity sheet per group. Direct students to use the chart to help them plan a story about how the disappearance of the keystone species changes their relationships. Ask students to consider the point of view of their animal, and remind them to refer to the concept map. Ask students to create sounds and gestures to personify their animals, such as a rabbit hopping about, a warbler flapping its wings, or a slithering snake. Circulate as students work, and use the Planning Questions to guide students in developing their stories and characters.

7. Have each group of students tell their story to the class to make clear how a wide range of animals can be affected by a single species and how their lives and needs are intertwined. Use the Questions for Discussion to debrief students. Emphasize how the concept map you recorded as a class helped them remember the information.

Planning Questions

- What character traits will your animal have?

- Describe the issue that the animal is faced with and how it will deal with it.

- What choices does the animal have in dealing with the dilemma?

- What props and gestures can you use to develop your character?

- Where will your story unfold?

- What will you see, smell, hear, and touch in this location?

- What dilemma does your animal encounter? What choices does he or she have in dealing with the challenge?

- How will you create empathy with your character?

Questions for Discussion

- How did you create a vivid character?

- How did the concept map we recorded as a class help you remember the information in the story?

- What are examples of other interdependent relationships?

- How did you use the interdependent relationships to help you develop your story?

- How did personifying an animal as it coped with the removal of a keystone species help you think about human relationships to animals and their environment?

- What story elements did you use to bring your story to life (e.g., character, setting, and dialogue)?

Personification *(cont.)*

Specific Grade Level Ideas

K–2

Instead of assigning the names of species for students to personify, give students pictures of the animals. (*At Home with the Gopher Tortoise: The Story of a Keystone Species* provides great pictures in the back of the book.) Have students tell improvised stories, focusing on the personification of animals in their environments and their need to find food and shelter within a habitat.

Students could also personify a seed as it grows into a plant, an object as it moves across different surfaces, or an object as it spins or rocks back and forth.

3–5

Draw a concept map of the storytelling experience, encouraging students to improvise and add twists and turns to their story. Students could add interdependent connections to the story that they research independently. Encourage students to recognize the interdependence within food webs and discuss the connections. Be sure to have students consider the point of view of the animal they personify. What is the human impact on their character?

Students could also personify part of a machine that has been lost or the potential uses of a tool.

6–8

Students can investigate species external to the web in the story. Each student can become a character in the story that would create tension and suspense on the existing relationships within the ecosystem. Encourage students to invent character behaviors based on their observations and the emotional responses of their classmates. Investigate animals that students are familiar with that live in local ecosystems (schoolyard, watershed, forest). Discuss the connections between different interdependent relationship cycles. As students personify each animal, ask them to consider the animal's point of view. How does their character view humans? How do humans affect their character and its environment?

Students can personify a molecule of water as it travels through an environment or changes from one state to another (gas to liquid), or a fossil as it is formed.

Name _____ Date _____

Fact Finding and Observations

Directions: As you listen to the story, fill in the chart to record information about your animal that will help you create a story.

Animal	
Animal Characteristics	
Habitat (food, shelter, water, space)	
Interdependent Relationships	Animal 1
	Animal 2
	Animal 3

Name _____   Date _____

Story Planner

Directions: Use this chart to plan your story.

Storytelling Technique	Story Elements
Personification: How will you personify your animal? List its character traits. How will you use voice, gesture, and props to show these traits?	**Beginning:** Introduce your animal. Describe the animal in its original habitat, including the location, sounds, water, food, and shelter.
	Middle: Describe how and why the keystone species was removed. What is your animal's reaction? Consider Introducing other characters, such as humans, animals, or inanimate objects. How are they affected?
	End: Describe how you survive. Who or what helps you? How do you feel? Where do you go?

Points of Entry

Model Lesson: Seed Journey Story Enders

Model Lesson Overview

This strategy can be used at any point in a story. In this lesson, students enter a story at the end and work backward. They begin with a plant taking root and work backward to weave a tale about the journey of the seed from its parent plant to its final destination. Students observe seeds closely and conduct research as they develop their seed characters. Developing their story also brings forth the interconnectedness of living things and the distinct characteristics of ecosystems as seeds disperse and grow, encountering forces beyond their control that can take them to new places.

Standards

K–2

- Knows that living things are found almost everywhere in the world and that distinct environments support the life of different types of plants and animals

- Knows that living things go through a process of growth and change

- Knows setting, main characters, main events, sequence, narrator, and problems in stories

3–5

- Knows that an organism's pattern of behavior is related to the kinds of organisms present in their environment

- Knows that organisms have distinct structures that serve specific functions in growth and survival

- Knows the factors that affect the types of organisms an ecosystem can support

- Understands elements of character development in literary works

6–8

- Knows relationships that are mutually beneficial in an ecosystem

- Knows relationships that are competitive in an ecosystem

- Creates characters, environments, and actions that create tension and suspense

Points of Entry *(cont.)*

Materials

- Assorted seeds
- Book about seeds and how they propagate
- *Seed Character Development* (page 191, seeddevelopment.pdf)
- Magnifying glasses (*optional*)

- Large paper for storyboards
- *Storyboard Planner* (page 192, storyboardplanner.pdf)
- *Sample Storytelling Techniques* (page 190, storytechniques.pdf)

Preparation

Gather various seeds from your local environment or home and ask students to do the same. Seeds should be easily accessible in a market or the local surroundings (popcorn, dandelion, etc.) Display seeds in the classroom and select one seed, such as a dandelion seed, to develop a sample story with students. Locate an image of the ecosystem in which your chosen seed grows. Locate a book about seeds and how they propagate. *Seeds* by Ken Robbins is an excellent resource for inspiration. Additional suggestions are provided in the Specific Grade Level Ideas.

Procedure

1. Ask students to identify seeds they know, including the ones they brought from home. Ask students to tell what they know about seeds. Discuss how seeds grow and travel, who or what might help them travel, how far they travel, and by what methods seeds can travel. Ask students how they could find information about dispersal of particular seeds and their respective habitats. Read aloud a book about seeds, and ask students to imagine that they are one of the seeds.

2. Share your selected seed, such as a dandelion seed, and an image of the ecosystem in which it grows, such as a school sports field. Ask students to imagine that they are that seed and tell the story of its journey, starting with the end and working backward. Have students consider the following questions: How did the seed arrive in that field—by a human, by an animal, or by the wind? Where did it come from? Trace as many steps back as you can until you arrive at the seed separating from its parent plant. As students offer their ideas, record the events of the story as they tell it and display them so that students can refer to them throughout the lesson.

3. Once the full story is recorded, add details and tell it to students from the perspective of the seed, or invite them to tell the story from the seed's perspective.

4. Have students observe the collection of seeds in the display area and classify them based on how they disperse (by wind, by water, by animals, etc.). If necessary, have students use reference materials to determine this information.

Points of Entry *(cont.)*

5. Divide students into small groups and have each group choose a seed from the class collection to research and write a story about. Try to cover all seed dispersal methods among the groups of students. Provide each group with an image of the ecosystem in which their seed grows to use as a story ender or have students select an image.

6. Distribute the *Seed Character Development* (page 191) activity sheet to students. Have students closely observe their seeds (use magnifying glasses when appropriate) and research the plant to figure out what conditions it needs to grow and develop. Students should also research seed anatomy, method of release or travel, and special conditions for propagation, such as fire or animal digestion. Direct students to gather and document their seed character research on the *Seed Character Development* activity sheet.

7. Ask students to imagine that they are the seed they have been researching. Tell them they are going to create an adventure story that tells of their seed's life journey. In this story, they should include information they found in their research. Discuss the elements of storytelling, including *setting*, *character*, *plot*, *action*, and *dialogue*. Ask students how they might bring the story to life in a sensory way. They should begin their story at the end and work backward to create the full story. Then, they can retell the story from beginning to end.

8. Distribute a large sheet of paper to students and have them fold it twice to create four sections to use as a storyboard. Distribute the *Storyboard Planner* (page 192) activity sheet to help them develop their storyboard. Remind students to begin filling in the *Storyboard Planner* at the end and work backward.

9. Distribute the *Sample Storytelling Techniques* (page 190) activity sheet. Have students practice telling their stories with partners, using various voices and intonations to express emotion.

10. Invite students to share their stories with the whole class. Use the Questions for Discussion to review and articulate the connections between science and storytelling.

Questions for Discussion

- What did you learn about your seed through the development of your character?

- What impact did the environment have on your seed character?

- How did the relationships in your seed's habitat support the plot in your story?

- What decisions did you need to make in the creation of your story and how were these decisions informed by your research?

- What story elements did you use as you shared the experience of your character?

Points of Entry *(cont.)*

Specific Grade Level Ideas

K–2

The Tiny Seed by Eric Carle is a great resource for students as it provides a model of a story that tracks the seed's trajectory. This strategy invites students to refine their intuitive understanding of *living* versus *nonliving* and explore and articulate how seeds grow, develop, and reproduce. Students' research will be observational as students notice, make sense of, and articulate what they see. This strategy can be used to investigate the life cycle of any living creature or natural phenomenon, such as the water cycle.

3–5

Seeds by Ken Robbins is a great book that includes seed details and entices the imagination. Have students collect seeds at home and in their local environment, classify them based on particular characteristics, use magnifying glasses to observe details, and research the parent plant and where it grows. Have students gather data on plant dispersal and growth in a classroom setting or outdoors and communicate the meaning of the data. Have students use this data to develop a concrete and well-rounded character and establish the setting. They can then tell a story that follows the trajectory of the seed until it grows into a plant. Remind students to describe the habitat, the weather, and the interactions with other things, both living and nonliving. This strategy can also be used to have students explore other living things whose transformation is easily observable and can translate into a story with multiple points of entry, such as butterflies or frogs.

6–8

Have students search for seeds at home, research the plant's habitat, and track the many factors the seed interacts with on its journey. Students can use this knowledge to build compelling settings for their stories. Have students consider the following: What does the seed do for other living beings, and in which ways is the seed useful to other creatures? What effect does the seed have on its habitat and vice versa? What competitive and beneficial relationships exist between this seed and other organisms in its environment? How are these relationships visible in the story plot and the interactions between characters? This strategy can also be used to investigate the trajectories of other living things such as insects or tadpoles that go through significant transformation in both shape and eating habits and that also have a significant environmental impact. This strategy can also be used to investigate other natural cycles, such as the life of a star.

Name _____   Date _____

Sample Storytelling Techniques

Find ways to engage the audience. Invite the audience into the story by posing a question.

Repeat lines to heighten audience awareness and add dramatic interest.

Allow your voice to hold emotion, reflecting the intensity of what is happening in the story as it unfolds.

Use facial expressions and eye contact to allow the audience to feel as though they are connected to the story.

Alter the tempo of your speech. Slowing down and speeding up language can intensify the story as the audience is brought along with the pace.

Use descriptive details to help the audience picture the story as it is being told.

Name _____   Date _____

Seed Character Development

Directions: Fill in as much information about your seed character as you can. You can draw, write, or do both.

What kind of seed are you?

What do you look like?

How do you travel?

Where do you grow?

What kind of conditions do you require?

Name _____   Date _____

Storyboard Planner

Directions: Imagine you are a seed. Use the planner to help tell your life story. Start at the end and work backward. Then, tell the story from beginning to end.

Beginning: Time and Place	**Middle: Dangerous Opportunity**
You are in your original habitat with your parent plant. What is your name? How do you feel? What is the habitat like? What sounds can you hear? What is the temperature? Who else is there? _____ _____ _____ _____ _____	*You separate from your parent plant.* How do you separate? What do you notice? Where do you go? What happens? Is there anyone else involved? _____ _____ _____ _____ _____
Middle: Seed Journey	**End: Arrival and Transformation**
You are traveling to your new home. Where do you go? How do you travel? Who or what helps you along? How does that make you feel? _____ _____ _____ _____	*You arrive at your destination.* What beneficial or competitive forces exist here? How does this place transform you? How do you feel here? What does this place look like? Feel like? Sound like? Who else is here? _____ _____ _____

Retelling

Model Lesson: Folktales and Sustainable Agriculture

Model Lesson Overview

In this lesson, students investigate a traditional folktale that reflects how different cultures use biodiversity in agriculture. Students investigate the scientific principles identified in the folktale and determine the most important aspects to retell while adding their own interpretation and language to integrate scientific explanations reflected in the folktale.

Standards

K–2

- Knows that Earth materials consist of solid rocks, soils, liquid water, and the gases of the atmosphere
- Reads folktales appropriate to grades K–2
- Uses different voice level, phrasing, and intonation for different situations

3–5

- Knows that all organisms (including humans) cause changes in their environments, and these changes can be beneficial or detrimental
- Reads folktales appropriate to grades 3–5
- Understands similarities and differences within and among literary works from various genre and cultures

6–8

- Knows ways in which organisms interact and depend on one another through food chains and food webs in an ecosystem
- Reads mythology appropriate to grades 6–8
- Uses appropriate verbal and nonverbal techniques for oral presentations

9–12

- Understands the interrelationship of agriculture with the environment and natural resources
- Knows ways in which humans can alter the equilibrium of ecosystems, causing potentially irreversible effects
- Summarizes and paraphrases complex, implicit hierarchic structures in informational texts

Retelling *(cont.)*

Materials

- Collection of different versions of the folktale "The Three Sisters"

- Index cards

- *Retelling Plan* (page 198, retellingplan.pdf)

Preparation

The American Indian story of the Three Sisters is about corn, squash, and beans that grow together and support one another. The corn serves as a stalk for the beans to hold on to and the squash crawls underneath, providing shade to prevent weeds from growing. The beans in turn support the fertility of the soil. This practice of intercropping is widely used in organic agriculture. There are other folktales from around the world that include this same concept.

Conduct an Internet search for different versions of the American Indian legend of the Three Sisters, or select a folktale that similarly discusses gardening, collaboration, nutrition, and agriculture.

Select multiple versions of the Three Sisters tale (or the folktale of your choice) to share with students and practice reading them aloud. Pick four events in the story and write them on four index cards. These will serve as cues for you to remember the storyline as you tell it to students. Practice telling the story, using your four cue cards.

Review the principles of organic agriculture. A great online source is the International Federation of Organic Agriculture Movements (IFOAM) (http://www.ifoam.org/). This website has a wide range of information about organic agriculture and its impact on the environment. Think of ways in which the folktale includes traditional practices that are now accepted as scientifically sustainable practices. Additional suggestions are provided in the Specific Grade Level Ideas.

Procedure

1. Introduce oral storytelling to students by explaining that stories are told and retold across cultures for a variety of reasons: to entertain, to educate, to preserve history, to share tradition, to question, and to explain phenomena. Discuss with students how folktales have been told and retold over time and how stories have been passed orally from generation to generation. Ask students, "Do you think the details of the story stay the same each time they are retold, or do they change? Why?" Ask students what makes a compelling story. How might they adjust the way story elements are used to enhance the telling and engage the audience to feel as if they were part of the story (e.g., *character*, *plot*, *action*, and *dialogue*)? Ask them to think of stories they have heard more than once in their homes, communities, or classrooms, and ask them to consider how stories change with each retelling.

Retelling (cont.)

2. Tell students that they are going to experience storytelling through the oral tradition. The story elements will stay the same, but the details will evolve with each retelling. Explain that they will investigate a traditional American Indian folktale that represents contemporary agricultural practices.

3. Tell the story of the Three Sisters to students as practiced, or tell the folktale of your choice and share additional versions. Ask students to keep track of how each variation differs.

4. Ask students to consider what information stays the same in the different versions. Ask students to identify the scientific content in the tales. Does this change? Discuss with students what scientific processes are at work. Ask them to name as many scientific processes as they can in relation to the story. Record this information for students to refer to throughout the lesson.

5. Divide students into small groups and distribute the *Retelling Plan* (page 198) activity sheet to each group. Instruct groups to select one version of the story to retell. Have students reread the tale and mark the important parts that they will include in their retelling. Ask them also to mark the places where they can connect to specific scientific content. Then, have them complete the *Retelling Plan* activity sheet.

6. Walk around and monitor groups, reminding students that it is okay to leave out some details but to make sure they include key scientific details using current information. Tell students that in this type of retelling, the story is not fixed but shifts with each retelling. They should capture the essence of the story using their own interpretation.

7. Have groups retell their tale several times with other small groups.

8. Invite students to share their story with the whole class. Use the Questions for Discussion to debrief.

Questions for Discussion

- What did you notice about your story as you retold it again and again while integrating new scientific details?

- What changed in your retelling? What remained the same?

- How did retelling your story affect your ability and confidence as a storyteller? How did it solidify your scientific understanding of the concepts involved?

- Why would it be beneficial to tell the story to the next generation?

Retelling (cont.)

Specific Grade Level Ideas

K–2

Read picture books of folktales from various cultures and select one for the class to retell together or in small groups. Students can draw simple pictures to represent the beginning, middle, and end of their story. As they retell, they can refer to the pictures.

Students can also discuss how humans can benefit from plants. Have them compile a cookbook of recipes that include any or all of the ingredients from the story.

This strategy can also be used to retell classic folktales about animals, such as The Tortoise and the Hare, and to consider how animals have varying characteristics. Many children's stories can be retold by integrating ideas about science, such as *The Very Hungry Caterpillar* by Eric Carle. Students can work as a group to tell the story along with what is happening scientifically.

3–5

Encourage students to try different leads as they retell their stories. For example, what would the effect be if they were to begin their oral retelling with a scientific question or by describing the setting? Ask students to consider how the seed or plant characters affect the soil character and how the plants function within the ecosystem to support one another's growth. They can integrate these scientific explanations into their retelling of the story.

This strategy can also be used with other kinds of stories to consider how nature works. Consider, for example, folktales and legends about the sun and the moon or about how mountains and lakes were formed. Browse the Internet for folktales or legends and add in the specific science content you are interested in addressing. For example, if you search for "folktales about water," you will find a wealth of stories from around the world related to water.

Retelling *(cont.)*

6–8

Gather a collection of folktales from various cultures that include similar examples of symbiotic plants that can benefit each other in a number of different ways. Examples include canopy coverage (shade-grown coffee), nitrogen fixation (beans), pest management (gardening with pest suppressors, such as pepper, or beneficial insects, such as ladybugs), and the way plants are positioned in the landscape. Ask students to include in their retellings information about how the various elements (light, water, soil, plants, humans, etc.) work to the benefit of one another and to also integrate contemporary scientific understandings.

Browse the Internet for "folktales for middle school" and select stories that focus on the impact of ecosystems on particular characters, such as animals.

9–12

Have students investigate how farms implement organic growing methods today. Explore how a particular method has changed or been influenced by technology or genetic engineering and how this will impact future generations. Have students rewrite the folktale with this information integrated. You can also invite students to write an original myth or folktale to respond to a present day issue and retell the story for others.

Browse the Internet for folktales related to any issue students may be interested in. Use technology such as video cameras to record the retellings and have students note the evolution of their storytelling over time.

Name _____ Date _____

Retelling Plan

Directions: As you create a new version of the folktale, work with your group to answer the following questions. Consider how to tell the story in a way that integrates science content while also making it exciting.

What are the important **narrative threads** that we need to include in the retelling?

What does the **character** want? What are the character's **traits** and **motivations**?

What are the important **scientific concepts** that we need to include in the retelling?

What **narrative details** are worth developing further in our retelling?

What **scientific details** are worth developing further in our retelling?

How will we **introduce** our story?

Collaborative Storytelling

Model Lesson: Investigating Systems

Model Lesson Overview

In this strategy, students develop a story by building on parts of the story offered by other students. Students investigate the systems that work together to provide them with what they need. By tracking back how a glass of water travelled to the classroom, students understand the multiple systems at play and develop a collaborative story about water moving through both natural and engineered systems.

Standards

K–2

- Knows ways that technology is used at home and at school

- Improvises dialogue to tell stories

- Knows setting, main characters, main events, sequence, narrator, and problems in stories

3–5

- Knows areas in which technology has improved human lives

- Knows that new inventions reflect people's needs and wants

- Understands the importance of characters' actions to the plot and theme

6–8

- Knows that technology cannot solve all human problems or meet all human needs

- Knows ways in which technology has influenced the course of history

- Understands elements of character development in literary works

9–12

- Knows that alternatives, risks, costs, and benefits must be considered when deciding on proposals to introduce new technologies or to curtail existing ones

- Understands the effects of author's style and complex literary devices and techniques on the overall quality of a work

- Uses a variety of verbal and nonverbal techniques for presentations and demonstrates poise and self-control while presenting

Collaborative Storytelling *(cont.)*

Materials

- Objects to serve as "talking sticks"

- *Refining the Story* (page 203, refiningstory.pdf)

- Drawing supplies (*optional*)

Preparation

Conduct research about water in your area and make a list of the multiple systems involved in bringing water into your classroom. This research will help you as you guide your students in tracking the systems that are involved. Additional suggestions are provided in the Specific Grade Level Ideas.

Procedure

1. Ask students to consider why they need water and discuss their ideas. Show students a glass of water and ask them how the water came to be in that glass. Explain that you poured it from the faucet, but how did it get to the faucet? With students, trace the process as far back as you can, including the pipes, the soil, the rain, etc. Record all the steps for students to refer to throughout the lesson.

2. Divide students into groups of 4 or 5, and have them research the various systems that are involved in getting water to homes, businesses, and schools, including both natural and engineered processes. Revisit the steps you recorded as a class to revise and add new information according to students' research.

3. Tell students that they will work together to develop a collaborative story about water, using what they know about water delivery systems. Divide students into groups of 4 or 5, and have each group select a "talking stick" to signify whose turn it is to add to the story. This can be any hand-held item, such as a ruler or a pencil. Ask students to discuss what makes a compelling story, including story elements such as *character*, *plot*, *setting*, *action*, etc.

4. Provide students with a prompt to spark a story that they will tell together. The prompt could be fantastic, such as, "An outer space creature keeps inhaling all the moisture from Earth's atmosphere, and as soon as more water evaporates, the creature takes it in." Or the prompt could be more practical, such as, "Chemical pollutants have spilled into the creek where local residents get their water."

Collaborative Storytelling *(cont.)*

5. Have students sit with their groups in a circle and give the talking stick to the first storyteller. This student begins the story by telling a few details. That student should then pass the talking stick on to the next student, who adds additional information before passing it on, and so forth. Student groups can decide to pass the talking stick around the circle or they can raise their hands when they have ideas to contribute.

6. After the story has been told one time through, distribute the *Refining the Story* (page 203) activity sheet to each group. Ask students to consider the characters, setting, and plot development of their stories, including the moment of crisis, resolution, and ending, and record them on the activity sheet. Then, ask students to add to, refine, or embellish their story and record these ideas as well.

7. Have students practice telling the new, improved version of their story, refining as needed. Ask them to consider who will tell which parts.

8. Have each group tell their story to the class. Use the Questions for Discussion to debrief.

Questions for Discussion

- How did developing the story collaboratively help you listen?

- How did you apply your new understanding In the context of the story plot?

- How did the character(s) develop as each student added to the story?

- How did the process of improvising a story as a group affect your understanding of storytelling, plot, characters, and story development?

Specific Grade Level Ideas

K–2

Have students focus on basic needs, such as water or food. Have students consider, for example, how an apple gets to homes. Who brings it home? How? Where did that person buy it? How did it get to the store? How did it get to the truck that brought it to the store? Have students tell the story from the point of view of the apple. It may be best to collaboratively tell the story as a whole class sitting in a circle. The story can also be developed into a collaborative storybook by giving each student one part of the story to illustrate. This strategy can be used to investigate systems for any need such as food, water, or clothes. The work can encompass social systems, technological systems such as cars, and natural ecosystems.

Collaborative Storytelling *(cont.)*

3–5

Have students investigate goods that have been packaged and that may include more than one ingredient. They can research what went into producing that good, the technologies used, the various ingredients from different places, and the costs, both environmental and economic.

6–8

Students can investigate the more complicated relationships between costs and benefits associated with getting something to the market. They can break into groups to investigate the various kinds of technologies that go into one product, such as communication technology, transportation technology, and agricultural technologies.

This strategy can be used to apply knowledge in any kind of system considering how something came to be, including natural phenomena, such as stars, black holes, and weather systems.

9–12

Students can investigate life-cycle assessments that include both energy and material inputs as well as environmental byproducts. A great resource for students to understand the process of life-cycle assessment is *Twinkie Deconstructed* by Steve Ettlinger. Students can develop stories in small groups about a particular product or technology and work together to consider how technology can help mitigate or eliminate some of the harmful unintended consequences. Students can focus their work on environmental science, technology, and/or engineering.

Name _____ Date _____

Refining the Story

Directions: After your first round of collaborative storytelling, fill in the chart to record the story. Then, add details to embellish the story. You can add more obstacles before the resolution or other pieces to make the story more engaging. Then, retell your new version of the story.

Story Title:
Nature of the problem:
Character(s):
Setting:
Moment of crisis (What happens in the story that creates tension with the characters?):
Resolution (How do the characters manage their way through the moment of crisis?):
Ending (What happens after the crisis is resolved?):

Visual Arts

#51086—*Strategies to Integrate the Arts in Science*

Visual Arts

Understanding Visual Arts

The importance of images and visual media in contemporary culture is changing what it means to be literate in the 21st century. Today's society is highly visual, and visual imagery is no longer supplemental to other forms of information. New digital technologies have made it possible for almost anyone to create and share visual media. Yet the pervasiveness of images and visual media does not necessarily mean that individuals are able to critically view, use, and produce visual content. Individuals must develop these essential skills in order to engage capably in a visually oriented society. Visual literacy empowers individuals to participate fully in a visual culture.

—Association of College & Research Libraries (2011)

We are bombarded with images on a daily basis, and although we have become more skilled at reading the nontextual representation of ideas, our visual-literacy abilities need to develop further. Why, then, is education so often text based? Working with images can provide opportunities for students to observe, notice details, and make meaning. Visual work can communicate nuances that words cannot. In this section, we see how students can use visual art as a language that is more unstructured than text.

Particular to visual arts is hands-on work with various materials. Visual artists use their art in many ways—to create visual narratives, observe, explore patterns, translate, represent concepts, and juxtapose ideas using visual communication. Using the elements of art—*line, form, shape, color, texture,* and *pattern*—students can investigate and create visual representations of ideas. They can also create images as a way to tell what they know.

Integrating the visual arts is a way to help students see and express scientific principles visually. Incorporating visual imagery into your science lessons, as in any other academic content area, can help make scientific concepts more tangible, accessible, and engaging (Dacey and Lynch 2007).

When students process visual information as well as verbal, they are using different parts of the brain. Allan Paivio suggests that learning can be expanded by the inclusion of visual imagery, allowing for what he termed "dual coding" (quoted in Reed 2010).

Moving between visual and scientific concepts can develop representational fluency and enhance students' ability to work with symbol systems. The visual arts are a natural fit with the sciences as images allow students to work in new ways with ideas of shape, scale, relationship, patterns, and more. As students translate scientific ideas into visual form, they engage their imagination and utilize both creative and critical thinking. All curricular areas have visual aspects, so providing students with the opportunity to work with multiple representations of content is easy to incorporate and will allow students new ways to engage with and access scientific ideas.

Visual Arts (cont.)

Strategies for Visual Arts

∿ Visual Narrative

In this strategy, students create and arrange images in sequence to tell a story or create a narrative. The story can be told through images alone, or the pictures can interact with text. Students' understanding of curricular content is enhanced as they create visual narratives that demonstrate and/or apply their learning. Often, creating a visual narrative makes it easier for students to grasp connections and clarify their thinking, which they can then translate into text. Students can illustrate scientific concepts, translating their understanding into visual form.

Visual narratives can culminate in the creation of simple books, digital image essays, magazines, storyboards, comics, and other formats that are easy to make. This allows students to compose content, applying and articulating their knowledge in new ways. Teaching artist and researcher Wendy Strauch-Nelson (2011) notes that the students "seemed drawn to the complementary relationship between the linear style of words and the layered nature of images" (9).

∿ Visual Experimentation

Experimentation is one of the key building blocks of visual art. Artists work with multiple ideas and materials with an element of free play that allows them to investigate and discover ways in which materials can interact with each other. In her research on arts organizations, Shirley Brice-Heath discusses the language used by artists and students as they talk about "What if?," "How about," and "Could we try this?" types of questioning (1999). It is through playing with materials to see "what if" that imaginative solutions to artistic problems can be developed. Science and engineering require manipulating materials to see how they function. Art invites students to apply that knowledge gleaned from experimentation in a playful manner as they create works that use scientific understanding in interesting and unusual ways.

∿ Visual Patterns

Artists often work with patterns. *Pattern* is considered one of the fundamental communication elements in the visual-arts principles of design. These design elements include *line*, *shape*, *form*, *texture*, *pattern*, and *color*. Through the visual arts, students can demonstrate a variety of curricular concepts by creating and manipulating patterns. Working with patterns can guide observations, and shifting patterns can generate interest and curiosity. Students can track and document patterns in the world through artistic representations that capture cycles of change. In the sciences, students can use visual patterns to deepen and extend their understanding of how biological and physical elements are shaped.

Visual Arts *(cont.)*

๛ Representation

Students investigate the ability of the visual arts to communicate information and ideas in compelling ways, to direct our attention, and to add layers of meaning. When students represent scientific findings through visual art, they translate their understanding of data into new forms, taking ownership of ideas and engaging with symbolism and metaphor.

David McCandless (2010) notes in his TED talk that we are overwhelmed by information and what he calls "data glut." He suggests that we work with representing data in new ways that prompt us to use our eyes. In this strategy, students create visual work, such as visual essays or infographics, to depict information.

๛ Mixed Media

This strategy allows students to experiment with putting a range of materials together in new ways. Students manipulate materials, experiment with the juxtaposition of materials, and create two- or three-dimensional pieces such as mobiles, collages, assemblages, dioramas, and digital installations. Students test and explore ideas in experiential, hands-on ways; make choices about how they will use materials to communicate; and explore cause-and-effect relationships in the process of working with different media. The use of multiple representations is essential to the development of flexible scientific strategies. This interpretive exploration will draw other themes. The construction of three-dimensional pieces requires students to interpret and explore ideas visually.

Visual Narrative

Model Lesson: 'Zines ROCK!

Model Lesson Overview

In this lesson, students work with teachers to create visual narratives called *'zines*. 'Zines (short for "magazine" and pronounced ZEEN) are small, handcrafted reproducible booklets. Students find rocks in their own neighborhoods, classify them, observe them, draw them, and represent them in a variety of ways. In groups, students create a visual narrative and story about their rocks, which will form their science 'zines.

Standards

K-2

- Knows that rocks come in many different shapes and sizes
- Uses art materials in a safe and responsible manner

3-5

- Knows that smaller rocks come from the breakage and weathering of larger rocks and bedrock
- Uses visual structures and functions of art to communicate ideas

6-8

- Knows that sedimentary, igneous, and metamorphic rocks contain evidence of the minerals, temperatures, and forces that created them
- Knows how the qualities of structures and functions of art are used to improve communication of one's ideas

9-12

- Knows that throughout the rock cycle, the total amount of material stays the same as its form changes
- Understands how the characteristics and structures of art are used to accomplish commercial, personal, communal, or other artistic intentions

Materials

- Magnifying glasses
- Soft pencils and dark pens
- Paper for rubbing
- Small sketchpads
- Digital photo cameras with macro or close-up ability (*optional*)

- *'Zine Template* (page 214, zinetemplate.pdf)
- Scissors
- Glue sticks
- *How to Assemble a 'Zine* (pages 215–216, assemblezine.pdf)

Visual Narrative *(cont.)*

Preparation

Look up the word "'zine" on the Internet. Survey different definitions to familiarize yourself with the culture of 'zines, and select some age-appropriate models to show students. The Small Science Collective has multiple 'zines on science available as PDFs. You can find other 'zine templates by looking up "'zine template" on the Internet. Refer to the Recommended Resources in Appendix C for additional resources.

Each group of students will need a collection of rocks that includes sedimentary, metamorphic, and igneous rocks. Students can work with a rock collection they bring in from home, or you can have them find rocks in the schoolyard. If they cannot find all three kinds of rocks in their immediate surroundings, supplement these rocks to make sure students familiarize themselves with all three kinds of rocks. Additional suggestions are provided in the Specific Grade Level Ideas.

Procedure

1. Ask students to bring in a few rocks from their neighborhood. Tell them to place each rock in a plastic bag with an index card that identifies where they found the rock.

2. Ask students to share what they know about one of the rocks they brought in. Ask questions such as, "Where did you find this rock? How do you think it got its shape?"

3. Divide students into groups of 2 or 3. Have students in each group combine their rock collections and classify the rocks they brought according to whether they are *sedimentary*, *metamorphic*, or *igneous*. Have each group present their rock findings to the class.

4. Explain to students what 'zines are. If students have made 'zines in the past, encourage them to bring in examples. Tell students that each group will be a 'zine production team, which will produce a 'zine telling a story about rocks.

5. Distribute a magnifying glass, a soft pencil, paper for rubbings, a small sketchpad, and drawing pens to each 'zine production team. Tell each team to make rubbings of their rocks and use the magnifying glass to look at the rocks close up and then draw them. Also, have them draw the rock outline from different angles using a dark pen. If available, have students use the macro feature on a digital camera to take highly detailed close-ups of the rocks.

6. Ask each group to give their rocks names and create a short narrative telling the story of their rocks. This story should include what they have learned about the rocks, including how they might have been formed and how they got their shape or texture.

Visual Narrative *(cont.)*

7. Distribute several *'Zine Template* (page 214) activity sheets to each group, along with scissors, glue sticks, and dark pens. Have students assemble their 'zines from the various visual elements and images they have produced. They could include images of the original index cards if desired. Students can also use text to supplement the information about their rocks.

8. Photocopy the 'zines, making enough for each student in class. Return the photocopied 'zines to their respective teams for students to fold and then redistribute to the class. Distribute the *How to Assemble a 'Zine* (pages 215–216) activity sheet and have each group fold their 'zines.

9. Have students distribute their 'zines to the class. If desired, you can assess students' work and submit them to the Small Science Collective (http://www.smallsciencezines.blogspot.com/) for publication, provide a copy of the 'zines to the school library, or have students share their 'zines with other grades to teach them about rocks.

10. Use the Questions for Discussion to debrief the activity.

Questions for Discussion

- What did you learn about rocks in your neighborhood?

- What forces do you think acted on the rocks in your story to give them their shape? How did you represent that visually in your 'zine?

- Do you think you can find lots of sedimentary, metamorphic, and/or igneous rock in your neighborhood? Why?

- What did you learn from drawing the rocks and creating images of them?

- What did you learn by putting your 'zines together? What would you do differently?

Specific Grade Level Ideas

K–2

Talk with students about the differences between rocks, pebbles, and sand. Have students work independently rather than in teams. Have each student create a single image of a rock and give it a name. Give students art supplies, such as colored pencils, crayons, or paints, sand, and glue, to create patterns around their rock pictures. Collect the images and combine them into a class book to create a visual narrative.

If working on a unit about birds or wildlife, have students draw images of birds or wildlife they see in their area.

Visual Narrative (cont.)

3–5

Have students concentrate on the effects of erosion and weathering in creating rock shapes. Students can make their story about the process of a rock weathering and becoming smaller, perhaps becoming part of the soil. Give each group an 8.5" × 11" sheet of paper that is folded in half. Have them create their story on just the inside two panels. Have each group create a separate part of the rock story and put them together in sequence and compile the various sections into a class book. Alternatively, have one student in each group create a page and have each group assemble their pages into a short 'zine.

This strategy can be used to explore any scientific process, such as the change of seasons, natural cycles, etc.

6–8

Students can go into the details of the various kinds of rocks and learn about and find evidence of various processes that affect rocks, such as the minerals, temperatures, and forces that created them.

Have each student develop a 'zine about a different planet, asteroid, comet, or meteor, and then trade 'zines.

9–12

Provide students with more complex 'zine templates (see the Recommended Resources in Appendix C for more ideas) to develop more sophisticated stories that may not necessarily be linear.

Students could also develop 'zines around the history of science and technology.

Name _____ Date _____

'Zine Template

Directions: Use this template to design your 'zine. The numbers (1–8) indicate the order of the pages for your 'zine. Fold a sheet of blank paper along the dotted lines shown on this template. Then, write and/or illustrate your narrative in the boxes. Remember to write/illustrate in the direction of the number in each box on the template.

2	1 (front)
3	8 (back)
4	7
5	6

Name _____ Date _____

How to Assemble a 'Zine

Directions: Follow the steps to fold your story into a 'zine.

1. Design your 'zine, using the *'Zine Template.*

2. Hold your 'zine design portrait and then fold it in half lengthwise. Use scissors to cut the 'zine as shown. Be careful to not cut beyond the indicated area.

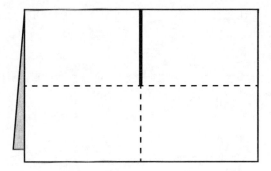

3. Unfold the 'zine design again. There should be a cut in the center.

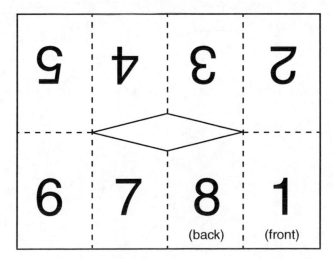

Name _____   Date _____

How to Assemble a 'Zine (cont.)

4. Then, fold your 'zine design landscape so all of the pages are on the outside as shown.

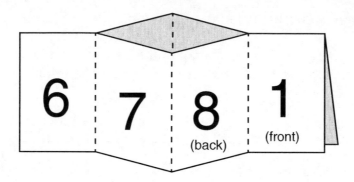

5. Pinching both sizes of the 'zine design, push inward so that a diamond shape is created from the cut section.

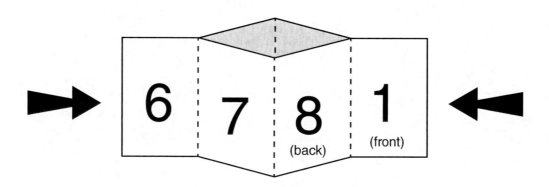

6. Fold the 'zine design so the pages go in the order of your narrative.

7. Your 'zine is complete!

Visual Experimentation

Model Lesson: Light Investigations

Model Lesson Overview

Experimentation is used extensively in both science and visual art. In this lesson, students experiment with light and shadow, using a range of materials. After this period of experimentation, students apply their knowledge as they transform lamps, flashlights, mirrors, and other objects into light sculptures.

Standards

K-2

- Knows that light travels in a straight line until it strikes an object
- Knows that learning can come from careful observations and simple experiments
- Knows how different materials, techniques, and processes cause different responses from the viewer

3-5

- Knows that light can be reflected, refracted, or absorbed
- Understands that specific artworks can elicit different responses
- Knows how different materials, techniques, and processes cause different responses from the viewer

6-8

- Knows that light interacts with matter by scattering
- Knows that light interacts with matter by absorption
- Understands how one's own artwork may elicit a variety of responses
- Knows how the qualities and characteristics of art media, techniques, and processes can be used to enhance communication of experiences and ideas

Materials

- White sheet, white paper, or bare white wall for screen
- Flashlights
- Sketchbooks and pencils
- *Light Experiment Documentation* (page 222, lightexperiment.pdf)
- Hand-held mirrors
- Transparent objects, such as color film sheets, plastic, water, bubbles (*optional*)
- Examples of shadow art
- Construction supplies such as wire, fishing line, construction paper, clay, tape

Visual Experimentation *(cont.)*

Preparation

Conduct an Internet search for images of "shadow art" and select examples to share with students. Shadow art by artists Christian Boltanski and Kumi Yamashita are good examples. Select a bare wall in your classroom or hang a white sheet or large roll of paper on a wall to create a white backdrop. Be sure it is large enough for all students to work with, or you can create multiple backdrops to make the space larger. Experiment with making your own shadow piece in your classroom to ensure that all the variables will work (the level of darkness in the room, the distances, the space, etc.).

Review the physics of light so you can help explain to students what is happening as they experiment with light. Additional suggestions are provided in the Specific Grade Level Ideas.

Procedure

1. Divide students into groups of 3 and distribute flashlights, sketchbooks, and the *Light Experiment Documentation* (page 222) activity sheet. Make sure the room is dim enough to track the light of a flashlight. Have one student in each group point light from a flashlight toward the white screen. Have a second student track the trajectory of the light by drawing an invisible line with his or her finger, or, to make this more concrete, have students use yarn to make the trajectory visible. Have the third student sketch what is happening on the *Light Experiment Documentation* activity sheet. Explain how light waves are travelling from point A (the flashlight) to point B (the screen).

2. Distribute hand-held mirrors and direct students to deflect the light and make it go in a different direction. Ask them to experiment with different angles. Tell students to track the angle of the light and document what they see on the *Light Experiment Documentation* activity sheet. Discuss what is happening with the light waves and ask students to predict what would happen if they placed certain materials in the light trajectory.

3. Have students experiment with placing different materials in the light trajectory. Depending on age and accessibility, provide transparent plastic, water, bubbles, crystals, clear film of various colors, and objects that may be solid or transparent. Ask students to experiment with holding the objects and the light at different angles and from different distances. Tell students to document at least two additional experiments on the *Light Experiment Documentation* activity sheet.

4. Ask students to experiment further and document what they see by considering shape, size, color, and the light source in their sketchbooks. Have students use lines to record the trajectory of the light toward the screen and to represent where they see light traveling to as well as the shapes the light makes on the screen or floor (if lit from above).

Visual Experimentation *(cont.)*

5. Share your selected examples of shadow art. Ask students what they see and what they notice. Ask questions such as, "What kinds of images do the light and shadow make? What do those images make you think of? Do they remind you of anything in your own life? How do you think you might feel if you were alone in the room with the shadows?"

6. Tell students that they will now make their own artwork by using light and shadow. Make construction materials available, such as wire, fishing line, construction paper, clay, and tape. Tell students they are free to create their shadow art using any of the available materials.

7. Have students turn on their flashlights and darken the room. Allow time for students to experiment with objects and ideas. If students are having trouble getting started, suggest that they cut shapes from construction paper and experiment with ways of holding them in the light. They will need to find a way to anchor shapes, such as attaching them to wires stuck in clay or by hanging them with fishing line. Use the Planning Questions to help students develop their work.

8. Provide a predetermined amount of time for students to edit and develop their pieces. Have them create sketches of their finished pieces in their sketchbooks.

9. Hold a class gallery walk around the room, lighting only one piece at a time. Have students sketch each piece in their sketchbooks, noting the trajectory of light in each. Use the Questions for Discussion to debrief.

10. Because these works are temporary, document students' shadow art by photographing or videotaping each piece, if possible.

Planning Questions

- What is your artwork about?

- What emotion or idea do you want your piece to convey (mystery, quiet, reflection, fun, sadness, etc.)?

- How might you create shadows with sharp edges?

- How might you create shadows with soft edges?

- Do you want it to be interactive? Do you want it to move?

- How will you use distance of objects in light to communicate ideas?

- How can you use your learning through experimentation (distance of objects, light angles, light sources, object opacity, etc.) to achieve your desired effect?

Visual Experimentation *(cont.)*

Questions for Discussion

- What is your shadow work about and how did you decide on that topic?

- What did you notice about shadows as an artist? As a scientist?

- How can light and shadow affect the atmosphere in a room?

- What did you learn about how light behaves by creating your shadow piece?

- How might you make a shadow piece if you were working only with natural light?

Specific Grade Level Ideas

K–2

Discuss light, shadow, and reflection with students, and then allow students to experiment with using their bodies to make shadows. If using a projector, students can get near and far from the projector to see how their shadows get bigger and smaller. Students can make shadow puppets by cutting out paper shapes and mounting them on craft sticks. Instead of focusing on the angles of light, students can draw what they see. Have students work either in small groups (each group can create puppets of animals that live in various habitats) or as a whole class to create a single piece. Students can also experiment with making floating sculptures out of natural materials, paper, or plastic building blocks tied to string and investigate how the objects move by pulling, pushing, blowing, etc.

This strategy can be used to have students investigate gravity by experimenting with sculptures made with rocks found outside.

Visual Experimentation *(cont.)*

3–5

Ask students to make diagrams that show the angles at which light is refracted and to consider various ways in which light scatters. You can integrate engineering and other forces of physics by asking students to develop freestanding pieces and/or hanging pieces that move, creating shifting shadows. Extend these ideas to the solar system and how light interacts at that level with the sun, the moon, and satellites.

Students can experiment to develop a sculpture that applies their knowledge of other science content, such as water (looking at currents, flotation, sinking, balance in relation to weight, density, etc.). For floating sculptures that take into account currents, look at Andy Goldsworthy's film *Rivers and Tides* and his other works in nature. After viewing Goldsworthy's work, students can investigate environmental issues as they do ephemeral sculptures, experimenting with natural materials outdoors.

This strategy can be used to explore engineering by having students experiment with materials to create machines. They can also integrate sound and movement to investigate additional content.

6–8

Bring in more sophisticated notions of physics in terms of light by adding color as a variable and investigating light wave absorption, reflection, and scattering. This lesson provides a good foundation for learning about waves by having students work with an element that is visible. Extend this learning to sound waves and other kinds of waves.

Challenge students both in visual arts and engineering by having them make interactive work that integrates visual imagery by using projected images to communicate something specific about a particular topic, such as weather, the solar system, or heat and energy. Have students integrate emotion by creating a piece that transforms when viewers interact with it, making the viewer reflect on a particular environmental issue. Students can push the idea of mood if they wish to convey a sense of urgency or of hope, for instance.

Name _____   Date _____

Light Experiment Documentation

Directions: In each square, draw what you see. Include the light source, and follow its trajectory. Use lines to illustrate where the light goes.

Flashlight to screen	Flashlight to _____ to screen
Flashlight to _____ to screen. Add any additional turns the light might take.	Flashlight to _____ to screen. Add any additional turns the light might take.

Visual Patterns

Model Lesson: Artful Lens to Scientific Observation

Model Lesson Overview

Observation is used in scientific processes to create detailed records of objects or events as evidence and as visual art to document and represent objects, relationships, and ideas. In this lesson, students closely observe patterns in nature that touch on both scientific and artistic aspects. Students study a small pattern within a natural context, record and document the pattern as they draw it, and enlarge it using a grid. Students then put their enlarged pattern details together to create a large-scale pattern in a collaborative piece that includes all students' work.

Standards

K–2

- Records information collected about the physical world
- Knows how different materials, techniques, and processes cause different responses from the viewer

3–5

- Knows that scientists' explanations about what happens in the world come partly from what they observe (evidence), and partly from how they interpret (inference) their observations
- Understands what makes different art media, techniques, and processes effective (or ineffective) in communicating various ideas

6–8

- Knows that there is no fixed procedure called "the scientific method," but that investigations involve systematic observations, carefully collected, relevant evidence, logical reasoning, and some imagination in developing hypotheses and explanations
- Uses appropriate tools and techniques to gather, analyze, and interpret scientific data
- Understands what makes different art media, techniques, and processes effective (or ineffective) in communicating various ideas

9–12

- Evaluates the results of scientific investigations, experiments, observations, theoretical and mathematical models, and explanations proposed by other scientists
- Applies media, techniques, and processes with sufficient skill, confidence, and sensitivity that one's intentions are carried out in artworks

Visual Patterns *(cont.)*

Materials

- Natural materials such as moss, bark, rocks, leaves, shells, pinecones, grasses, feathers, and insects

- *Viewfinder Frame* (page 228, viewfinderframe.pdf)

- *Observation Drawing Template* (page 229, drawingtemplate.pdf)

- Scissors

- *Magnification Grid* (page 230, magnificationgrid.pdf)

- Art supplies, such as colored pencils, markers, pastels, paints, etc.

Preparation

Browse the Internet for artwork that features patterns, and select examples to share with students. Pattern artwork can be found in the work of Andy Warhol, the sand patterns of Andres Amador, the snow art of Simon Beck, and the Swarm Intelligence Collaborative Drawing Project.

Using the directions in the Procedure, create an example of a gridded image to show students. Think of patterns you can use as examples to get students started, such as patterns easily seen in leaves, flowers, starfish, or snowflakes. Also, look at more abstract examples, such as the DNA sequence, taxonomic relationships, migration patterns, or food webs. Consider patterns created by humans to explain natural patterns and make things run more smoothly, such as a week, month, year, or season.

Collect natural materials, such as leaves, rocks, or pinecones for students to work from, or make plans to go outside as a class to collect materials. Additional suggestions are provided in the Specific Grade Level Ideas.

Procedure

1. Discuss the repetitive aspect of patterns and ask students to brainstorm places where they see patterns. These may include patterns in the built environment, such as brick patterns in houses or patterns in fences. Encourage students to consider where patterns exist in nature. They can look around the classroom, at their own skin for patterns, or go outside to find patterns in their environment.

2. Distribute the *Viewfinder Frame* (page 228) and the *Observation Drawing Template* (page 229) activity sheets to students and tell them they will be doing an observational drawing. Point out that the square on the *Observation Drawing Template* activity sheet is the same size as the square on the *Viewfinder Frame* activity sheet.

Visual Patterns *(cont.)*

3. Have students cut out the square on the *Viewfinder Frame* activity sheet and use the hole as a window to look at and frame patterns they observe in their surroundings. Students should use the *Viewfinder Frame* to frame a small piece of a pattern in nature so that it becomes an abstract cropped image. Then, have students reproduce the pattern they see on the *Observation Drawing Template* activity sheet. Ask them to notice where each element of the pattern (lines, dots, textures, etc.) is in relation to what they see in the *Viewfinder Frame*. Tell them to capture the pattern as accurately as possible on the *Observation Drawing Template* activity sheet.

4. Ask students to look at their drawings. Are they fairly accurate? How are they different from what they see? Is there anything they can add to make them more accurate? Invite students to refine their pieces by comparing the original pattern in nature against their drawings.

5. Tell students that they will now magnify their image by using a grid. In doing so, students can observe how scale has the ability to transform a pattern in a way that allows for creative design possibilities. Distribute the *Magnification Grid* (page 230) activity sheet and tell students to draw each section of the pattern from the *Observation Drawing Template* in an equivalent square on the *Magnification Grid*. When they are done, they will have a magnified version of their original pattern.

6. Ask students to check for accuracy and revise as necessary. Once their magnified patterns are complete, photocopy them and set them aside.

7. Distribute art supplies and ask students to transform the pattern on their *Magnification Grid* activity sheet to reflect an emotion or a scientific idea while maintaining the accuracy of the marks. They can add color, make lines darker or lighter, increase the contrast, etc. Tell students that they should transform their drawing to create an aesthetically interesting image imbued with a sense of interest and emotion. Share the selected examples of pattern art to inspire students.

8. Have students work together to create a display of all students' work on a classroom bulletin board or wall.

9. Next to the classroom display they have created, ask students to create a parallel display, using the photocopied versions of their original drawings. By doing this, students can see the pattern created with the accurate black and white drawings against the pattern created with their transformed pieces. Use the Questions for Discussion to debrief.

Visual Patterns *(cont.)*

Questions for Discussion

- How did the *Viewfinder Frame* help you see differently?

- Can anyone tell where the pattern came from? How did you figure it out?

- How does scale or magnification play a role in your observation?

- How did transforming the pattern into a new art piece make it different from the original pattern?

- What happened to the patterns when they were part of the class display?

- How are the two grids different (i.e., the grid displaying photocopied work and the grid displaying the transformed work)?

- How does art help you understand a sense of patterns in nature?

Specific Grade Level Ideas

K–2

If possible, take students outside to look for patterns in nature. Students can gather leaves and look at tree trunks and other natural elements. Have students use the *Viewfinder Frame* activity sheet to find and view a pattern in nature. If students find patterns that have texture such as rocks, they can do crayon rubbings instead of line drawings. Students can also glue natural objects (leaves, twigs, flowers, etc.) to sheets of paper to represent their patterns.

3–5

Have students use magnifying glasses to search for patterns that are not easily noticed by the naked eye. Ask them to select a pattern, view it under the magnifying glass, and frame it with their *Viewfinder Frame*. Have students draw the magnified image on the *Observation Drawing Template* before enlarging it with the *Magnification Grid*. Ask students to think about how they could bring out some of the elements that they see by emphasizing a particular element with color or by making elements darker and more prominent.

Students can use this strategy to observe, record, and transform any visual element of scientific study such as landscape patterns, skin texture (pores and hairs), plant life, insects, or rocks.

Visual Patterns *(cont.)*

6–8

Have students use a microscope to significantly magnify small natural elements (e.g., insects and leaves) and draw the visual patterns they see.

Students can also look at patterns in the built environment and consider how various patterns support structures, such as bridges and walls.

9–12

Encourage students to look for patterns in nature and notice how the patterns are used in engineering for functional purposes (patterns found in nature used as a foundation for the design of a bridge or a building). You can challenge students to find patterns in functional engineering and consider how these designs originated. Ask if the original idea could have come from observation. Invite students to think about how patterns can be transformed and expanded using other strategies (fractals, biomimicry, etc.). *Biomimicry: Innovation Inspired by Nature* by Janine M. Benyus is a great resource for this. Have students find patterns in nature and experiment with the scale of the patterns to transfer ideas into the design and engineering of functional objects.

Name _____ Date _____

Viewfinder Frame

Directions: Cut out the square and use this sheet of paper as a window to look at patterns in nature.

#51086—*Strategies to Integrate the Arts in Science* © *Shell Education*

Name _____ Date _____

Observation Drawing Template

Directions: Draw what you see in the *Viewfinder Frame*. Draw the pattern as accurately as you see it in your *Viewfinder Frame*, noticing where each form and line is in the frame.

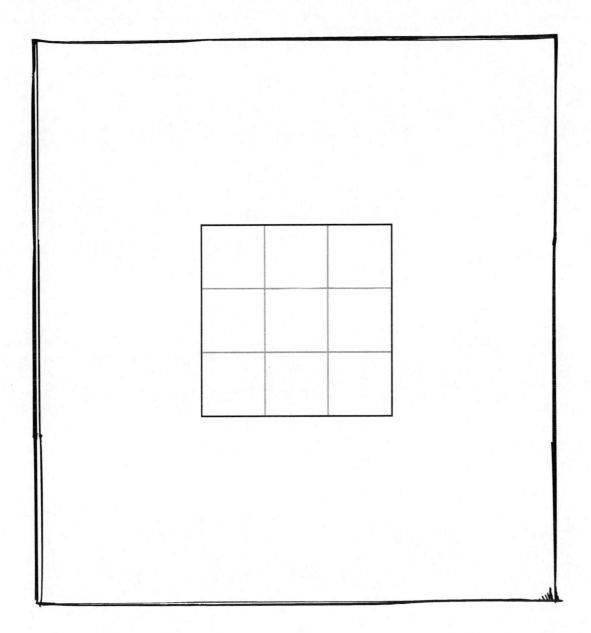

Name _____ Date _____

Magnification Grid

Directions: Look at your drawing on the *Observation Drawing Template*, and transfer the marks in each small square into the equivalent large square on this grid. Try to make it as accurate as possible.

Representation

Model Lesson: Technology and Environmental Impact

Model Lesson Overview

In this lesson, students collect, analyze, classify, and organize disposable objects in order to investigate their function and impact in home and school environments. Students collect the disposable items their families and schools use over the course of one week and transform them into visual artwork that elicits an emotional response as it represents the impact of disposable objects in our environment.

Standards

K–2

- Knows that people can design and make objects and systems to solve a problem and to improve the quality of life

- Knows that man-made materials, products, and systems can affect the environment adversely, yet there are things that can be done to circumvent this process

- Understands how different compositional, expressive features, and organizational principles cause different responses from the viewer

3–5

- Knows that technologies often have costs as well as benefits and can have an enormous effect on people and other living things

- Understands how different compositional, expressive features, and organizational principles cause different responses from the viewer

6–8

- Understands the ways in which human-induced changes in the physical environment in one place can cause changes in other places

- Understands what makes various organizational structures effective (or ineffective) in the communication of ideas

9–12

- Knows that alternatives, risks, costs, and benefits must be considered when deciding on proposals to introduce new technologies or to curtail existing ones

- Understands how the characteristics and structures of art are used to accomplish commercial, personal, communal, or other artistic intentions

Representation *(cont.)*

Materials

- Examples of trash art and found object art
- *Object Classification* (pages 236–237, objectclassification.pdf)
- Large sheets of cardboard or poster board
- Tape, glue, or staplers
- Measuring tapes
- *Impact Data Questionnaire* (page 238, impactdata.pdf)

Preparation

Conduct an Internet search for images of "trash art" and select examples of found object art to share with students. Good examples include Gabriel Orozco's *Sandstars* and *Astroturf Constellation*—part of his larger Asterisms exhibition—and the work of Paul Matosic. If desired, search for and select images and videos about the Great Pacific Garbage Patch to show students.

Consider the space you want to use for the installation. This could be inside the classroom, including the floor and/or walls, or, with appropriate permission, this could extend beyond your classroom into school hallways.

Ask students to collect disposable objects at home for one week. You can also ask students to gather all the disposable things they use in school throughout the week. All objects should be clean and dry before beginning the activity. Additional suggestions are provided in the Specific Grade Level Ideas.

Procedure

1. Share with students the definition of *disposable*. Then, ask students to look around the classroom and think about their daily routines. What disposable materials do they use?

2. Ask students why they think anyone would design disposable objects. Are there objects we would want to use only once? Why? What are the benefits of disposable objects? What unintended impacts might disposable objects have on the environment?

3. Ask students where they think the objects go once they are used and thrown out. Discuss where many of the objects end up—in landfills or the ocean. If desired, share images, facts, or videos about the Great Pacific Garbage Patch. Share with students alternative solutions and conservation practices, including reducing consumption, or reusing or recycling products as well as using engineered alternatives such as biodegradable plastics made from plants.

Representation *(cont.)*

4. Explain to students that they will be developing artwork that represents the disposable objects they use throughout the course of one week. Share examples of the work of artists who use found objects. Ask students what they notice about the works. What elements do the artists use to organize the materials? Do they see any patterns? How do these installations make them feel? What are they about?

5. Distribute the *Object Classification* (pages 236–237) activity sheet to students. Have students gather the disposable objects they brought in, classify ten items, note them in the chart, and answer the questions. This will help them select classification criteria for their artwork.

6. Divide students into groups of 4 and provide them with space to experiment with various ways of laying out their disposable materials. Have them group together their objects, spread them out, and organize them based on one or two criteria described in the chart. Ask them to consider how certain patterns and colors may create emotion. Have students create their pieces by laying the objects on a large sheet of poster board. Objects can remain loose or be glued, taped, or stapled onto the poster board.

7. Show students the designated space for the installation of disposable objects. Ask groups to organize their pieces into a larger class piece. They can put their arranged pieces side-by-side, in a long line, or in a flowing shape to resemble a river or other formation.

8. Distribute measuring tape and the *Impact Data Questionnaire* (page 238) activity sheet to students. Ask them to look at the class piece, measure it, and record their responses to the questionnaire. Discuss and compare results.

9. Use the Questions for Discussion to debrief and develop a plaque that includes the title, the size, the materials used, the date, a short explanation of the creative process, and the meaning of the work.

Questions for Discussion

- What criteria did you use to organize your objects into one whole?

- What objects are in your artwork? What do they make you think of?

- Look at the whole piece. What do you notice? What does it make you think of?

- What did you learn about art, technology, and science from this process?

- What title would you give this art installation?

Representation *(cont.)*

Specific Grade Level Ideas

K–2

Ask students to think about particular situations that they are familiar with, such as a birthday party, and have them consider the many things that get thrown away afterward (wrapping paper, balloons, plastic goody bags, etc.). Have students focus on the functions of discarded objects and transform them into festive party supplies (e.g., making garlands with remnants of ribbons and wrapping paper cut into small shapes). Culminate with a class celebration that focuses on sustainable practices. Ask students to suggest what else they can do to minimize waste, such as using reusable cups and dishes or making decorations, tablecloths, or wrapping paper out of used paper or plastic.

This strategy can also be used to investigate classification of plants, rocks, or animals. Use pictures to represent things that are not accessible as objects, such as insects and birds.

3–5

Have students focus on the benefits of technology and its costs to the environment. They can compare reusable containers with disposable containers, and track their life cycle to compare costs and benefits of both types of containers. Students can also use this strategy to consider the volume of other manufactured goods, such as plastic toys. The work of artist Tara Donovan, who makes art out of large amounts of objects, such as buttons, tape, pencils, and polystyrene cups, is a good resource. Challenge students to take into account things we keep that we do not need.

This strategy can also be used to investigate the nature of scientific inquiry as it supports observation, classification, and data analysis. Students can use this strategy to represent unity and diversity within any population such as animals, insects, plants, or food. Or it can be used to represent weather by asking students to represent how much rain or snow falls in various areas using images of water drops or snowflakes.

Representation *(cont.)*

6–8

As an extension, have students investigate the effects of disposable objects in other places. For example, they can investigate natural habitats uninhabited by humans that end up full of our disposable garbage. They can investigate the North Atlantic Garbage Patch and develop work that focuses on the impact on the ocean and the coasts. With this focus, they can also learn about ocean currents and how they interact with human technology for better and for worse. *Tracking Trash: Flotsam, Jetsam, and the Science of Ocean Motion* by Loree Griffin Burns is a great book for this level. The strategy can also be extended to address human population and impact on any ecosystem.

Students can also investigate very small objects, such as germs or subatomic particles.

9–12

In addition to the 6–8 Specific Grade Level Ideas, have students identify the five major ocean gyres (the North Atlantic Gyre, the South Atlantic Gyre, the South Pacific Gyre, the North Pacific Gyre, and the Indian Ocean Gyre) and any respective garbage patches that result from ocean currents in those areas. Students can create visual representations that express the feelings and emotions of negatively impacted wildlife or ecosystems. After students identify the five major ocean gyres, have them conduct research to discover the different types of pollutants in each ocean gyre, comparing the gyre, the pollutants, and the surrounding human populations that contribute to the formation of these oceanic garbage patches.

Name _____   Date _____

Object Classification

Directions: Choose ten disposable objects and describe them in the chart. Experiment with organizing your objects according to one or two criteria. Then, answer the questions to help you determine the final organization of your objects.

Color										
Size										
Shape										
Reusable, Biodegradable, or Recyclable										
Material										
Function										
Object										

Name _____   Date _____

Object Classification *(cont.)*

1. Which objects have the greatest visual impact?

    _____

    _____

    _____

    _____

2. Which have the greatest emotional impact?

    _____

    _____

    _____

    _____

3. Which objects will you use in your final installation? Why?

    _____

    _____

    _____

    _____

4. What criteria will you use to organize them? Why?

    _____

    _____

    _____

    _____

Name _____   Date _____

Impact Data Questionnaire

Directions: Look at the final piece and answer the questions.

1. Measure the class installation. How much space does it take up?

> Our classroom installation measures _____ square feet.

2. How much space would an installation take up that includes disposable objects from all the classrooms in your school?

> (_____ number of classrooms in your school × _____ square feet of display per classroom)
>
> All the disposable objects in all the classrooms in our school would measure about _____ square feet.

3. How much space would an installation take up that includes the disposable objects from all schools in your city?

> (_____ number of schools in your city × _____ square feet of display per school)
>
> All the disposable objects in all the schools in our city would measure about _____ square feet.

Mixed Media

Model Lesson: Collage and the Changing Earth

Model Lesson Overview

In this lesson, students use mixed media to investigate and represent the earth and how it changes during geological processes. They use various materials to create diptychs that include before and after representations of a location and show the impact of forces that affect the earth, such as rain, deforestation, volcanic activity, global warming, and the movement of plate tectonics.

Standards

K–2	3–5
• Knows that there are different materials on Earth • Understands that a model of something is different from the real thing but can be used to learn something about the real thing • Experiments with a variety of color, textures, and shapes	• Knows how features on the Earth's surface are constantly changed by a combination of slow and rapid processes • Understands that models can be used to represent and predict changes in objects, events, and processes • Understands what makes different art media, techniques, and processes effective (or ineffective) in communicating various ideas

6–8	9–12
• Knows how land forms are created through a combination of constructive and destructive forces • Knows that models are often used to think about things that cannot be observed or investigated directly • Understands what makes different art media, techniques, and processes effective (or ineffective) in communicating various ideas	• Understands the concept of plate tectonics • Applies media, techniques, and processes with sufficient skill, confidence, and sensitivity that one's intentions are carried out in artworks

Mixed Media *(cont.)*

Materials

- *Planning Guide* (page 244, planningguide.pdf)
- *Diptych Template* (page 245, diptychtemplate.pdf)
- Heavy 11" × 14" construction or watercolor paper
- Scissors, glue, crayons, and/or colored pencils
- Other collage materials, such as construction paper, magazines, etc. *(optional)*

Preparation

Consider the geological forces you want students to investigate and browse the Internet for images of how the Earth's surface is affected by those forces. You can focus on natural forces, such as wind, water, melting glaciers, or volcanoes, or you can focus on human forces to investigate deforestation, construction, and overgrazing. Select both aerial and ground images to share with students for reference.

Gather art materials and cut sheets of 11" × 14" heavy paper in half the long way so there are strips of paper that measure about 5.5" × 14". Students will fold each strip in half so that they have two connected panels (like a two-page book).

Ideally, make your own diptych to share with students in order to foresee and resolve any potential glitches in the process. Additional suggestions are provided in the Specific Grade Level Ideas.

Procedure

1. Introduce students to forces that change the earth. Ask them if they have ever noticed ways in which the ground changes, such as when running water makes a path in loose soil. Share other examples that they may have seen, such as a bulldozer digging into the ground, and ask them if they can think of other ways in which the landscape changes.

2. Share images you gathered and discuss with students how various forces shape the landscape of the earth. Ask them to notice the marks on the landscape and consider how they were formed.

3. Tell students that they will be investigating a place affected by a particular force, and they will make *diptychs* to represent how the landscape has changed. Explain that a *diptych* is a work of art with two connected panels that form one complete piece. Tell students that one side of their diptychs will represent the landscape *before* change and the other side will represent the landscape *after* it has been transformed. Remind students that the earth changes constantly and they are to choose only two moments in time.

Mixed Media (cont.)

4. Distribute the *Planning Guide* (page 244) activity sheet to students and allow them to choose a place they will represent in their diptychs. Have them look at past and present images of their location by conducting research about the area. Direct students to use the *Planning Guide* to help them develop ideas for their diptychs.

5. Distribute the *Diptych Template* (page 245) activity sheet, and have students roughly sketch their idea.

6. Tell students that they will create their diptychs using the technique of *collage*. Explain that they will cut and/or tear apart materials and glue it to paper, overlapping pieces and creating texture to represent the earth.

7. Tell students that they will create texture and color for their collages by doing rubbings. Model this process by placing a sheet of white paper on a textured surface and coloring it with the side of a crayon or pencil to capture the texture. Tell students they can also paint, crumple, or tear paper in addition to using found textures, such as magazine paper, newspaper, or tissue paper. Allow time for students to plan their collages, using information from the *Planning Guide* activity sheet.

8. Distribute the 5.5" × 14" inch strips of paper to students. Have students fold their strips in half to create two sides that open like the pages of a book. Provide scissors, glue, and time for students to cut, tear, and glue materials to create their diptychs. Tell students they can also layer the paper to create a sense of volume or relief if they want to represent a raised surface from an aerial perspective.

9. Have students exhibit their finished diptychs on their desks. Then, take a gallery walk around the classroom to view the work. Use the Questions for Discussion to debrief and critique the work.

Questions for Discussion

- What shapes and textures do you see in the various collages?

- What materials were used to achieve the colors, shapes, and textures?

- What kinds of terrain and material do they represent?

- How are the two images in the diptych different from each other?

- How does having two images help you visualize the impact of the forces and the changes in the earth?

- Do any of the collages elicit an emotional response?

Mixed Media *(cont.)*

Specific Grade Level Ideas

K–2

Have students investigate what the earth is made of. Take students outside to look at the ground right beneath their feet. They can dig up and gather samples of the different things that make up the ground (soil, little rocks, some roots, etc.). Students can experiment with what happens when some of those elements interact with water (e.g., pouring soil and rocks into a clear water container). They can then experiment with materials, including natural objects from the earth, to create a collage that represents what the earth is made of. Students can also use collage to represent various forms of life with natural materials such as plants. And they can use this strategy to show different times in growth cycles of various plants or animals as well.

3–5

Students can focus on the multiple ways in which the earth gradually changes. For example, they can construct collages that represent weathering, erosion, or sediment created by atmospheric forces, such as wind or water. Students can also consider how each of these changes affects our experience on the planet. They can observe the phenomena at the beach and consider seashells or think about the weathering of soil if they live inland and look at how that affects not just humans but also animals. Have students consider what other art mediums would be useful to investigate and represent these points.

Students can also use this strategy to focus on the impact of technology on the changing earth.

Mixed Media (cont.)

6–8

Students can investigate plate tectonics by developing a diptych based on a particular place. Students can work in groups to investigate the geological phenomena that affect the Hawaiian Islands, Iceland, and the Rocky Mountains. Students should use deductive reasoning to determine which type of plate movement is involved and which type of boundary is created.

This strategy can also be used to develop models of other scientific concepts such as the lithosphere. Students can also focus on life sciences by imagining particular ecosystems to consider human impact on those environments. They can consider the impact on particular populations of animals or organisms by imagining them in their habitats before and after particular events.

9–12

Students can go into depth about the causes (e.g., heat and gravitational forces) and effects (e.g., earthquakes and volcanic eruptions) of plate tectonics. Have students collect images that represent a particular area of the globe to research. Their models could include two sides, one side representing Earth's surface that shows details, such as the boundaries of each plate, and one side including arrows that indicate the direction of its movement.

Students could also use this strategy to address specific short-term and long-term technological impacts in their local area. They can use this strategy as a way to investigate the potential impact of technologies that support the health and conservation of the earth by preventing erosion or by conserving energy.

Name _____   Date _____

Planning Guide

Directions: Research the area you will represent and fill in the chart. Use your research and the images you found to describe the location before and after the change.

Ecosystem or landscape: _____

	First image: before change	**Second image: after change**
Description of the ecosystem or landscape		
Forces that affect the landscape		
Natural elements (soil, rock, water, ice, etc.)		
Colors		
Textures		

Name _____   Date _____

Diptych Template

Directions: Sketch your collage. Then, use your sketch as a guide for selecting colored and textured paper to use on your diptych.

Before	After

References Cited

Albers, Donald J., Gerald L. Alexanderson, and Constance Reid, eds. 1990. *More Mathematical People: Contemporary Conversations*. New York: Harcourt Brace Jovanovich.

Andersen, Christopher. 2004. "Learning in 'As-If' Worlds: Cognition in Drama in Education." *Theory into Practice* 43 (4): 281–286.

Anderson, Lorin W., David R. Krathwohl, Peter W. Airasian, Kathleen A. Cruikshank, Richard E. Mayer, Paul R. Pintrich, James Raths, and Merlin C. Wittrock. 2000. *A Taxonomy for Learning, Teaching, and Assessing: A Revision of Bloom's Taxonomy of Educational Objectives*. Boston, MA: Allyn & Bacon.

Association of College & Research Libraries. 2011. "ACRL Visual Literacy Competency Standards for Higher Education." Accessed October 10, 2012. http://www.ala.org/acrl/standards/visualliteracy.

Baker, Beth. 2012. "Arts Education." *CQ Researcher* 22: 253–276.

Bamberger, Jeanne. 2000. "Music, Math, and Science: Towards an Integrated Curriculum." *Journal for Learning through Music* Summer 2000: 32–35.

Bellisario, Kerrie, and Lisa Donovan with Monica Prendergast. 2012. "Voices from the Field: Teachers' Views on the Relevance of Arts Integration." Unpublished manuscript. Cambridge, MA: Lesley University.

Brice-Heath, Shirley. 1999. "Imaginative Actuality: Learning in the Arts During the Nonschool Hours." In *Champions of Change: The Impact of the Arts on Learning*, edited by Edward B. Fiske. Washington, DC: Presidents' Committee on the Arts and the Humanities.

Burnaford, Gail, with Sally Brown, James Doherty, and H. James McLaughlin. 2007. *Arts Integration, Frameworks, Research, and Practice*. Washington, DC: Arts Education Partnership.

Cahill, Bryon. 2006. "Ready, Set, Write!" *Writing* 29 (1): 12.

Cappiello, Mary Ann, and Erika Thulin Dawes. 2013. *Teaching with Text Sets*. Huntington Beach, CA: Shell Education.

Carpenter, Siri. 2010. "Body of Thought: How Trivial Sensations Can Influence Reasoning, Social Judgment, and Perception." *Scientific American Mind* (January 2011): 38–45.

Center for Applied Special Technology, The. Accessed October 10, 2012. http://www.cast.org/about/index.html.

Collins, Anne M. 2012a. *50 Leveled Math Problems Level 5*. Huntington Beach, CA: Shell Education.

References Cited (cont.)

————. 2012b. *50 Leveled Math Problems Level 6*. Huntington Beach, CA: Shell Education.

Collins, Polly. 2008. "Using Poetry throughout the Curriculum." *Kappa Delta Pi Record* 44 (2): 81–84.

Coulter, Cathy, Charles Michael, and Leslie Poynor. 2007. "Storytelling as Pedagogy: An Unexpected Outcome of Narrative Inquiry." *Curriculum Inquiry* 37 (2): 103–122.

Dacey, Linda. 2012a. *50 Leveled Math Problems Level 1*. Huntington Beach, CA: Shell Education.

————. 2012b. *50 Leveled Math Problems Level 2*. Huntington Beach, CA: Shell Education.

————. 2012c. *50 Leveled Math Problems Level 3*. Huntington Beach, CA: Shell Education.

————. 2012d. *50 Leveled Math Problems Level 4*. Huntington Beach, CA: Shell Education.

Dacey, Linda, and Jayne Bamford Lynch. 2007. *Math for All: Differentiating Instruction, 3–5*. Sausalito, CA: Math Solutions.

Diaz, Gene, Lisa Donovan, and Louise Pascale. 2006. "Integrated Teaching through the Arts." Presentation given at the UNESCO World Conference on Arts Education in Lisbon, Portugal, March 8.

Donovan, Lisa, and Louise Pascale. 2012. *Integrating the Arts Across the Content Areas*. Huntington Beach, CA: Shell Education.

Dunn, Sonja. 1999. "Just What Is a Chant?" Accessed October 10, 2012. http://www.songsforteaching.com/sonjadunn/whatisachant.htm.

Elliott-Johns, Susan E., David Booth, Jennifer Rowsell, Enrique Puig, and Jane Paterson. 2012. "Using Student Voices to Guide Instruction." *Voices from the Middle* 19 (3): 25–31.

Gardner, Howard. 2011. *Frames of Mind: The Theory of Multiple Intelligences*. 3rd ed. New York: Basic Books.

Growney, JoAnne. 2009. "What Poetry Is Found in Mathematics? What Possibilities Exist for Its Translation?" *Mathematical Intelligencer* 31 (4): 12–14.

Hamilton, Martha, and Mitch Weiss. 2005. *Children Tell Stories: Teaching and Using Storytelling in the Classroom*. Katonah, NY: Richard C. Owen Publishers.

Heathcote, Dorothy, and Gavin Bolton. 1995. *Drama for Learning: Dorothy Heathcote's Mantle of the Expert Approach to Education*. Portsmouth, NH: Heinemann.

Herman, Corie. 2003. "Teaching the Cinquain: The Quintet Recipe." *Teachers & Writers* 34 (5): 19–21.

References Cited *(cont.)*

Hetland, Lois. 2009. "Nilaja Sun's 'No Child'... : Revealing Teaching and Learning through Theater." *Teaching Artist Journal* 7 (1): 34–39.

Hetland, Lois, Ellen Winner, Shirely Veenema, and Kimberly Sheridan. 2007. *Studio Thinking: The Real Benefits of Visual Arts Education.* New York: Teachers College Press.

Hourcade, Juan Pablo, Benjamin B. Bederson, and Allison Druin. 2003. "Building KidPad: An Application for Children's Collaborative Storytelling." *Software: Practice & Experience* 34 (9): 895–914.

Jenkins, Henry. 2009. *Confronting the Challenges of Participatory Culture: Media Education for the 21st Century.* Cambridge, MA: The MacArthur Foundation.

Jensen, Eric P. 2001. *Arts With the Brain in Mind.* Alexandria, VA: Association for Supervision and Curriculum Development.

———. 2008. *Brain-Based Learning: The New Paradigm of Teaching.* 2nd edition. Thousand Oaks, CA: Corwin Press.

Kennedy, Randy. 2006. "Guggenheim Study Suggests Arts Education Benefits Literacy Skills." *The New York Times*, July 27.

Kuta, Katherine. 2003. "And who are you?" *Writing* 25 (5): 30–31.

LaBonty, Jan. 1997. "Poetry in the Classroom: Part I." *The Dragon Lode* 75 (3): 24–26.

Lane, Barry. 1992. *After THE END: Teaching and Learning Creative Revision.* Portsmouth, NH: Heinemann.

Lyon, George Ella. 2010. "Where I'm From." Accessed March 2, 2010. http://www.georgeellalyon.com/where.html.

Marzano, Robert J. 2007. *The Art and Science of Teaching: A Comprehensive Framework for Effective Instruction.* Alexandria, VA: ASCD.

McCandless, David. 2010. "David McCandless: The beauty of data visualization." Filmed July 2010, TED video, 18:17. Posted August 2010. http://www.ted.com/talks/david_mccandless_the_beauty_of_data_visualization.html.

McKim, Elizabeth, and Judith W. Steinbergh. 1992. *Beyond Words: Writing Poems With Children: A Guide for Parents and Teachers.* Brookline, MA: Talking Stone Press.

National Research Council. 2012. *A Framework for K–12 Science Education: Practices, Crosscutting Concepts, and Core Ideas.* Washington, DC: The National Academies Press.

New, David. 2009. "Listen." National Film Board of Canada video, 6:21. Accessed October 10, 2012. http://www.nfb.ca/film/listen.

References Cited *(cont.)*

Norfolk, Sherry, Jane Stenson, and Diane Williams. 2006. *The Storytelling Classroom.* Westport, CT: Libraries Unlimited.

O'Neill, Cecily. 1995. *Drama Worlds: A Framework for Process Drama.* Portsmouth, NH: Heinemann.

Paquette, Kelli R., and Sue A. Rieg. 2008. "Using Music to Support the Literacy Development of Young English Language Learners." *Early Childhood Education Journal* 36 (3): 227–232.

Partnership for 21st Century Skills. 2011. Accessed October 15, 2012. http://www.p21.org/.

Perret, Peter, and Janet Fox. 2006. *A Well-Tempered Mind: Using Music to Help Children Listen and Learn.* New York: Dana Press.

President's Committee on the Arts and the Humanities. 2011. "Reinvesting in Arts Education: Winning America's Future Through Creative Schools." Accessed January 2, 2013. http://www.pcah.gov/sites/default/files/PCAH_Reinvesting_4web_0.pdf.

Reed, Stephen K. 2010. *Cognition: Theories and Application,* 8th ed. Belmont, CA: Wadsworth Cengage Learning.

Reeves, Douglas. 2007. "Academics and the Arts." *Educational Leadership* 64 (5): 80–81.

Rhode Island School of Design. 2011. "Gathering STEAM in Rhode Island." Accessed October 10, 2012. http://www.risd.edu/About/News/Gathering_STEAM_in_RI/.

Rinne, Luke, Emma Gregory, Julia Yarmolinskyay, and Mariale Hardiman. 2011. "Why Arts Integration Improves Long-Term Retention of Content." *Mind, Brain, and Education* 5 (2): 89–96.

Rose, Todd. 2012. "Learner Variability and Universal Design for Learning." Universal Design for Learning Series video, 15:36. http://udlseries.udlcenter.org/presentations/learner_variability.html.

Skoning, Stacey N. 2008. "Movement in Dance in the Inclusive Classroom." *TEACHING Exceptional Children Plus* 4 (6).

Stewart, Marilyn G., and Sydney R. Walker. 2005. *Rethinking Curriculum in Art.* Worcester, MA: Davis Publications.

Strauch-Nelson, Wendy J. 2011. "Book Learning: The Cognitive Potential of Bookmaking." *Teaching Artist Journal* 9 (1): 5–15.

Theodorakou, Kalliopi, and Yannis Zervas. 2003. "The Effects of the Creative Movement Teaching Method and the Traditional Teaching Method on Elementary School Children's Self-Esteem." *Sport, Education and Society* 8 (1): 91–104.

References Cited *(cont.)*

Walker, Elaine, Carmine Tabone, and Gustave Weltsek. 2011. "When Achievement Data Meet Drama and Arts Integration." *Language Arts* 88 (5).

Waters, Sandie H., and Andrew S. Gibbons. 2004. "Design Languages, Notation Systems, and Instructional Technology: A Case Study." *Educational Technology Research & Development* 52 (2): 57–68.

Yew, Jude. 2005. "Collaborative Narratives: Collaborative Learning in Blogosphere." Master's thesis, University of Michigan. DOI: 2027.42/39368.

Zull, James E. 2002. *The Art of Changing the Brain: Enriching Teaching by Exploring the Biology of Learning.* Sterling, VA: Stylus.

Note-Taking Tool for
Observational Assessment

Date: _____

General Notes							
Questions Asked							
Comments Made							
Student Name							

Arts Integration Assessment Rubric for Science

Student Name _____ Date_____

Skill	Beginning	Developing	Meeting	Exceeding
Demonstrates understanding of science concepts and skills				
Demonstrates understanding of art concepts and skills				
Communicates thinking clearly				
Demonstrates creative thinking				

Individual Observation Form

Student Name _____ Date _____

Shows understanding (Check all that apply)

_____ Makes representations or notes to understand more fully

_____ Talks with a peer to understand more fully

_____ Asks teacher questions to understand more fully

_____ Helps others to understand

Explains or justifies thinking (Check all that apply)

_____ Communicates thinking clearly

_____ Uses art forms, words, symbols, and writing to summarize thinking (Underline communication forms that apply)

_____ Uses content vocabulary

Takes it further (Check all that apply)

_____ Makes connections to previous learning

_____ Elaborates on artwork beyond expectations

_____ Suggests new science connections

_____ Creates multiple correct responses to task

Group Observation Form

Student Name _____ Date_____

Use this form to record scores, comments, or both.

Scores: 1—Beginning   2—Developing   3—Meeting   4—Exceeding

Suggests at least one appropriate task solution			
Works cooperatively			
Supports others in their learning			
Communicates clearly, uses correct vocabulary, and builds on the ideas of others			
Provides leadership/ suggestions to group			
Group Members			

Printed with the permission of Shell Education (Collins 2012a, 2012b; Dacey 2012a, 2012b, 2012c, 2012d)

Recommended Resources

Embodiment

Canadian Museum of Nature
http://www.youtube.com/watch?v=moITG5Q7zzI

Choreography

The Cornell Lab of Ornithology
http://www.birds.cornell.edu

Mantle of the Expert

Cornell Lab of Ornithology
http://www.birds.cornell.edu

Design Squad Nation
http://pbskids.org/designsquad/

Monologue

Roddy, Ruth Mae. 2000. *Minute Monologues for Kids: Contemporary Scene-Study Pieces for Kids.* Rancho Mirage, CA: Dramaline Publications.

Stevens, Chambers. 2009. *Magnificent Monologues for Kids 2: More Kids' Monologues for Every Occasion!* South Pasadena, CA: Sandcastle Publishing.

Sampling

The National Weather Service
http://forecast.weather.gov/

Scoring

Barbatuques. 2008. "Barbatuques." YouTube video, 2:42. Uploaded July 6, 2008. Posted by "Anton Umnitsyn." http://www.youtube.com/watch?v=XCzjk9PDHb4.

Burchfield, James. 2008. "James Burchfield plays (invisible) turntables." Filmed February 2003, TED video, 4:46. Posted October 2008. http://www.ted.com/talks/james _burchfield_plays_invisible_turntables.html/.

Recommended Resources *(cont.)*

McFerrin, Bobby. 2011. vimeo video, 1:08:26. April 22, 2011. http://vimeo.com/25170698.

International Body Music Festival
http://www.internationalbodymusicfestival.com

Instrumentation

The Young Person's Guide to the Orchestra
http://listeningadventures.carnegiehall.org/ypgto/index.aspx

Rhyme and Rhythm

Chute, Marchette. 1957. "The Drinking Fountain." In *Around and About: Rhymes by Marchette Chute*. New York: E. P. Dutton.

dePaola, Tomie. 1988. "The Secret Place." In *Tomie dePaola's Book of Poems*. New York: Putnam Juvenile.

Nash, Ogden. 2007. "Children's Party." In *The Best of Nash Ogden*. Chicago, IL: Ivan R. Dee Publisher.

Prelutsky, Jack. 2006. *The Beauty of the Beast: Poems from the Animal Kingdom*. New York: Young Books for Young Readers.

Shelley, Percy. 1956. "The Cloud." In *Shelley: Poems*. New York: Penguin.

Silverstein, Shel. 1981. "Messy Room." In *A Light in the Attic*. New York: HarperCollins.

Prompt

NISE Network
http://nisenet.org/

Philadelphia Science Festival
http://www.philasciencefestival.org/

Personification

Dunphy, Madeleine. 2010. *At Home with the Gopher Tortoise: The Story of a Keystone Species*. Berkeley, CA: Web of Life Children's Books.

Points of Entry

Carle, Eric. 2009. *The Tiny Seed*. New York: Little Simon.

Robbins, Ken. 2005. *Seeds*. New York: Atheneum Books for Young Readers.

Recommended Resources *(cont.)*

Retelling

Carle, Eric. 1987. *The Very Hungry Caterpillar*. New York: Philomel Books.

International Federation of Organic Agriculture Movements (IFOAM)
http://www.ifoam.org/

Collaborative Storytelling

Ettlinger, Steve. 2007. *Twinkie Deconstructed*. New York: Hudson Street Press.

Visual Narrative

Kozdras, Deborah. 2012. "Zines for Kids: Multigenre Texts About Media Icons."
Accessed February 28, 2013. http://www.readwritethink.org/classroom-resources
/lesson-plans/zines-kids-multigenre-texts-1013.html.

"Rocks and Minerals." 2011. Teachers' Domain. Accessed February 28, 2013.
http://www.teachersdomain.org/resource/idptv11.sci.ess.earthsys.d4krom/.

Wrekk, Alex. 2002. *Stolen Sharpie Revolution*. Portland, OR: Microcosm Publishing.

Small Science Collective
http://www.smallsciencezines.blogspot.com/

Todd, Mark, and Esther Pearl Watson. 2006. *Whatcha Mean, What's a Zine? The Art of Making Zines and Mini-Comics*. New York: Graphia.

Zine Writer's Guild
http://zinewritersguild.wikia.com/

Visual Experimentation

Christian Boltanski Shadow Art
http://www.salzburgfoundation.at/content/blogcategory/99/210/lang,en/

Goldsworthy, Andy. 2001. *Rivers and Tides*. DVD. Directed by Thomas Riedelsheimer. San Francisco, CA: Microcinema International USA.

Kumi Yamashita Shadow Art
http://www.kumiyamashita.com/light-and-shadow/

Visual Patterns

Andy Warhol
http://www.warhol.org/

Andres Amador
http://www.andresamadorarts.com/

Recommended Resources *(cont.)*

Benyus, Janine M. 1997. *Biomimicry: Innovation Inspired by Nature.* New York: William Morrow.

Simon Beck
http://trendland.com/simon-becks-snow-art/

Swarm Intelligence Collaborative Drawing Project
http://www.lyndaschlosberg.com/blog/2012/swarm-intellegince-collaborative-drawing-project/

Representation

Burns, Loree Griffin. 2007. *Tracking Trash: Flotsam, Jetsam, and the Science of Ocean Motion.* New York: Houghton Mifflin.

Gabriel Orozco's Asterisms
http://www.guggenheim.org/new-york/exhibitions/past/exhibit/4775/

Paul Matosic
http://www.matosic.org.uk/

Tara Donovan
http://www.acegallery.net/artistmenu.php?Artist=8

Contents of the Digital Resource CD

Page Number	Resource Title	Filename
N/A	Correlation to the Standards	standards.pdf
30	Embodied Movement Planning Guide	embodiedguide.pdf embodiedguide.doc
31–32	Six Qualities of Movement Reference Sheet	sixqualities.pdf
33	Phase Change Narrative	phasechange.pdf phasechange.doc
39	Moving Statue Documentation Form	movingstatue.pdf movingstatue.doc
N/A	Solar System Model 1	solarsystem1.pdf
N/A	Solar System Model 2	solarsystem2.pdf
44	Planetary Movement	planetary.pdf planetary.doc
49	Scientific Observation Notes	scientificnotes.pdf scientificnotes.doc
50	Choreographic Notation Sheet	notation.pdf notation.doc
56	Magnet Experimentation Documentation	magnet.pdf magnet.doc
57	Nonlocomotive Movement Reference and Notation	nonlocomotive.pdf nonlocomotive.doc
70	Zoo Director Memo	zoomemo.pdf zoomemo.doc
71	Brainstorming Guide	brainstormingguide.pdf brainstormingguide.doc
72	Presentation Guide	presentationguide.pdf presentationguide.doc
77	Design Engineer Script	engineerscript.pdf engineerscript.doc
78	Engineering Evidence Chart	evidencechart.pdf evidencechart.doc
84	Gallery Walk Observation Sheet	gallerywalk.pdf gallerywalk.doc
90	Affecting History	affectinghistory.pdf affectinghistory.doc

Contents of the Digital Resource CD *(cont.)*

Page Number	Resource Title	Filename
91	Sample Monologue 1: Jane Goodall	monologue1.pdf
92	Sample Monologue 2: Jane Goodall	monologue2.pdf
93	Monologue Planner	monologueplanner.pdf monologueplanner.doc
97–98	Explore the Character	explorecharacter.pdf explorecharacter.doc
108	Sound Observation Chart	soundobservation.pdf soundobservation.doc
109	Sound Categories	soundcategories.pdf soundcategories.doc
115	Sampling and Sound	samplingsound.pdf samplingsound.doc
120	Human Percussion Notation	humannotation.pdf humannotation.doc
125	Instrument Design	instrumentdesign.pdf instrumentdesign.doc
130	Tree of Life	treelife.pdf
140–141	Dialogue Poem Examples	dialogueexamples.pdf
142	Two Voices Poem Plan	twovoicesplan.pdf twovoicesplan.doc
147	Where I'm from Scientifically Examples	wherefromexamples.pdf
148	Where I'm from Scientifically Planner	wherefromplanner.pdf wherefromplanner.doc
153	Science Concept Poem Examples	scienceconcept.pdf
154	Rhymes and Rhythms Planning Guide	rhymesrhythm.pdf rhymesrhythm.doc
155	My Science Concept Poem	myscienceconcept.pdf myscienceconcept.doc
160	Poetry Word List	poetrywordlist.pdf poetrywordlist.doc
165	Cinquain Examples	cinquainexamples.pdf
166	Word-Count Cinquain Planner	cinquainplanner1.pdf cinquainplanner1.doc

Contents of the Digital Resource CD *(cont.)*

Page Number	Resource Title	Filename
167	Parts of Speech Cinquain Planner	cinquainplanner2.pdf cinquainplanner2.doc
168	Syllables Cinquain Planner	cinquainplanner3.pdf cinquainplanner3.doc
178	Scientist Interview	scientistinterview.pdf scientistinterview.doc
179	Story Planning Questions	storyquestions.pdf storyquestions.doc
184	Fact Finding and Observations	factfinding.pdf factfinding.doc
N/A	Concept Map 1	conceptmap1.pdf
N/A	Concept Map 2	conceptmap2.pdf
185	Story Planner	storyplanner.pdf storyplanner.doc
190	Sample Storytelling Techniques	storytechniques.pdf
191	Seed Character Development	seeddevelopment.pdf seeddevelopment.doc
192	Storyboard Planner	storyboardplanner.pdf storyboardplanner.doc
198	Retelling Plan	retellingplan.pdf retellingplan.doc
203	Refining the Story	refiningstory.pdf refiningstory.doc
214	'Zine Template	zinetemplate.pdf
215–216	How to Assemble a 'Zine	assemblezine.pdf
222	Light Experiment Documentation	lightexperiment.pdf lightexperiment.doc
228	Viewfinder Frame	viewfinderframe.pdf
229	Observation Drawing Template	drawingtemplate.pdf
230	Magnification Grid	magnificationgrid.pdf magnificationgrid.doc
236–237	Object Classification	objectclassification.pdf objectclassification.doc

Contents of the Digital Resource CD (cont.)

Page Number	Resource Title	Filename
238	Impact Data Questionnaire	impactdata.pdf impactdata.doc
244	Planning Guide	planningguide.pdf planningguide.doc
245	Diptych Template	diptychtemplate.pdf diptychtemplate.doc
251	Note-Taking Tool for Observational Assessment	notetaking.pdf
252	Arts Integration Assessment Rubric for Science	assessmentrubric.pdf
253	Individual Observation Form	individualform.pdf
254	Group Observation Form	groupform.pdf

Acknowledgments

We are extremely grateful for the dedication and hard work of the many individuals who have shaped this book. As such, we would like to give special thanks to the following individuals:

Federico R. Poey, Ph.D., for a life of science inspiration at the dinner table, in the garden, in the corn fields, in the ocean, and just about everywhere

Camila Lissa Telemaque, for her hard work drawing and writing, and for asking lots of questions

Guy Michel Telemaque, for all that made the work possible

Bertha A. Poey, for listening and encouraging

Marco Tulio Lopez, for being a great support and reflective sounding board throughout the process

Leyli Lopez Weber, for inspiring the foundation of the work to connect the two creative worlds of art and science

Rayetta Fischbach, for encouraging exploration and observation throughout life

Mary Brooks, for being a positive reviewer within an art education context from a scientific perspective

Notes

#51086—Strategies to Integrate the Arts in Science © Shell Education